Faith, Hope and Mischief

Faith, Hope and Mischief

Tiny Acts of Rebellion

Andrew Graystone

CANTERBURY
PRESS
Norwich

© Andrew Graystone 2020

Published in 2020 by Canterbury Press
Editorial office
3rd Floor, Invicta House,
108–114 Golden Lane,
London EC1Y 0TG, UK
www.canterburypress.co.uk

Canterbury Press is an imprint of Hymns Ancient & Modern Ltd
(a registered charity)

Hymns Ancient & Modern® is a registered trademark of
Hymns Ancient & Modern Ltd
13A Hellesdon Park Road, Norwich,
Norfolk NR6 5DR, UK

Scripture quotation taken from The Holy Bible, International
Children's Bible copyright 1986, 1988, 1999, 2015 by
Tommy Nelson™, a division of Thomas Nelson.
All rights reserved.

Cover image © Bilal Chawala 2019

British Library Cataloguing in Publication data

A catalogue record for this book is available

from the British Library

978 1 786 22259 6

Music typeset by Andrew Parker

Typeset by Regent Typesetting
Printed and bound by
4edge Limited, UK

Dedication

The place where I'm most at home in the world doesn't exist for 51 weeks of the year. It is the Greenbelt Festival, a celebration of arts, faith and justice that takes place over the August Bank Holiday weekend every year. I have attended Greenbelt virtually every year for four decades. In that time, people have come and gone, ideas have been tested, and mistakes have been made. The festival has moved location half a dozen times and changed almost beyond recognition, and so have I. Along the way, the Greenbelt community has shaped me, challenged me, loved me and held me. This book is offered with thanks to Greenbelt and its people.

Contents

Preface

This is a book of stories. All of them are true, and all of them happened to me, but those are the only things that these stories have in common. Some of them are quite short, and others are longer. Some of them are about really important things that happened to me – big decisions and turning points. Others are about the smallest things that happened in the briefest of moments.

What links them is what you might call Everyday Activism. Everyday Activism is about living in the world in an engaged way, in the simple belief that things could be a bit better than they are. The role of Everyday Activism is not to save the planet or to change the world. Either of those things would be such a burdensome, impossible job for any human that they would most certainly be broken in the task. The task of the Everyday Activist is simply to find the good things that are going on, and nurture them. This is not one vast project, but a million tiny acts of rebellion – saying no to the way the world is, and yes to another way. Everyday Activists believe in taking risks, making mischief and doing small things that make a big difference. Everyday Activism is transgressive. It consists in small acts of resistance. It is about lighting candles in dark rooms, encouraging people who have lost hope, touching people who feel untouchable and making connections that enable power to flow. Everyday Activists are wide-eyed wonderers. We hang out with the wrong kind of people – people who are not like us. We do things our mother wouldn't approve of. We skirmish with injustice and laugh in all the wrong places. In particular we laugh at ourselves. Above all, we believe that – despite evidence to the contrary – the world's story is going to end well.

I am an Everyday Activist. These are my stories. What are yours?

Where there is no love, put love, and you will find love.

St John of the Cross

I

What Do You Do?

Last week my mum rang me with a question that had been bugging her. 'I was talking to one of the ladies at the Mothers' Union, and she asked me what you do. What should I have told her?' I knew straight away that when she said, 'What do you do?' she wasn't looking for me to say, 'I walk the dog most nights and I'm handy with a screwdriver.' She was talking about work ... and specifically what pays the rent. And I honestly didn't really know what to say. I do a bit of broadcasting and a bit of journalism; I teach a bit; I'm doing some study. I think of myself as an Everyday Activist – but what does that actually mean?

What I mean by that is that in all the things I do and all the people I meet, I see it as my job to try to find where goodness is at work – and if I can, to point it out to other people. I do all sorts of different jobs to pay the rent. But you won't be surprised to know that no one actually employs me to be an Everyday Activist. I guess that's what I'd call my vocation.

Except ... I'm a bit wary of the idea of vocation. It's a word religious people tend to use a lot. Often, the suggestion is that there's a job out there that you're called to do, and you have to find it if you want to be happy. It's a bit like the idea that there's one person out there somewhere among the seven billion of us who is Mr or Ms Right for you, and you have to find them if you want a happy life. I don't buy that at all. Sure, there are quite a lot of people who could make you distinctly unhappy. But there are quite a few who would make you reasonably happy too ... certainly more than one. It's not just who you marry, but who you are with your partner – that's what makes the difference. Same with work. If you can make a job out of doing the thing you love, that's great, but lots of people don't have that luxury. Lots of us just have to find whatever work we can and try to make something of it. What's more, lots of us have to spend huge proportions of our time doing things that don't really count as work at all because they are not paid, but they just need to be done. I'm up for changing the world, really I am. I'm more than willing to be Greta Thunberg or Nelson Mandela or Malala Yousafzai. But first I have to cook the dinner/pick up the kids from school/find a way to stop the water coming through the bathroom ceiling. Plus, I need to sleep. Because somehow, before I've even started on my saving the planet agenda, I find myself exhausted by the mundane stuff of life. If I'm going to be an activist, I will need to be an Everyday Activist. I will need to work out my deepest values, and get the shopping in at the same time.

So, what about vocation? I think of it like a Venn diagram. In one circle is the person you most truly are: your skills and your interests, and most importantly the things you really care about; the things that stir your passion. In the other circle is the world, with all its opportunities and all its many many needs. You will find your vocation in the place where the person you are deep down overlaps with what the world most needs. If you can hit that sweet spot, you'll find a rhythm where your self dissolves easily into the tasks you have to do.

Vocation is not just about paid work. That's really import-ant to know, because getting a job is not as simple as deciding what you're called to and walking into it. We don't have all those choices available to us. But we can choose what sort of person we are, and to some extent how we spend our time and who we spend it with. I have a feeling that if I am ever called to account for my life by God, God won't ask me, 'Why were you not Prime Minister or President or Archbishop?' God will ask me, 'Why were you not Andrew?'

I knew we would end up talking about God. We always do, but as soon as we do, we run into difficulty. The only thing we can use to talk about God is words, and words are human creations, so they are always going to be inadequate. Worse than that, every word you use is far smaller than the God you are trying to describe. In the novel *A Passage to India* by E. M. Forster, one of the characters refers to 'poor little talkative Christianity'. Ouch! That stings. I've spent countless hours of my life in churches, and most of what we did there was talk. I've contributed more than enough of those words myself. I wonder if the sum total of my words has actually shrunk people's image of God. Sometimes I think that the most effective thing the Church could do to evangelize the nation is to shut up.

The whole business of listening to God is not as easy as it sounds. Not everybody 'hears' God's voice in a way that's clear enough to put God down as a reference on an application form. But everybody has a place that's right for them. If you want to find what God is calling you to, my suggestion is that you listen really honestly to your self, and your heart's deep longing; then listen hard to the world, and its deep need. And what you hear there – that will be God speaking to you. The place where those two things meet, whether it's being the prime minister or pressing flowers, that place is where you are called to be.

The Russian playwright Anton Chekhov is reputed to have said, 'Don't tell me the moon is shining; show me the glint of light on broken glass.' It gave rise to one of the first rules for writers and film directors: 'show, don't tell'. And yet here I am, contributing another pile of words to the world. My excuse is that I want to tell you some stories. My stories are nothing special. They are certainly no more valuable than yours. I am a middle-aged, middle-class, white Christian man who was brought up not to make a fuss. I admire the people who do great things that change the whole world. I'm in awe of Malala, and Greta and Mandela, but if I'm honest, great people sometimes make me aware of my own smallness. The fact that I recycle my jam jars and switch off the car engine at traffic lights is simply not going to save the planet, and the knowledge of that sometimes makes me feel hopeless. As a result, I have tried to cultivate an attitude of seriousness in life – but also of nonsense.

George Orwell said, 'Every joke is a tiny revolution'. At the very least, a joke disrupts the settled order of our everyday lives. The joke starts, and for a moment we're carried into a world of possibilities, before being dropped from a height into familiarity. Laughter brings down the towers of pomp and power – sometimes our own. That's why no one likes being the butt of a joke. Where Christians are persecuted it is because they declare that Jesus, not Caesar, is Lord. And Caesar can't bear being laughed at.

That's why laughter is one of the sharpest tools in the Every-day Activist's toolkit. It has so many uses. If it is used carefully, laughter can deflate the pompous and cut them down to size. It can empower people who have been squashed or abused. Sometimes it can do both at the same time. And if all else fails, laughter has power to heal deep wounds. I have been privileged to lead a few funerals in my time, and I always think they have done their job if there is laughter somewhere along the way.

Of course, laughter has to be used carefully, or it can hit the wrong target. Sometimes comedians talk about the vital differ-ence between 'punching up' – laughing at people who are more powerful than you – and 'punching down' – laughing at people who are vulnerable.

I try to sense the gravity of each moment, and the extra-ordinary privilege of what the poet Mary Oliver called my 'one wild and precious life'. Life is a solemn business – but then you get your foot stuck in the drawer of a drinks vending machine. Looking back over my life from the vantage point of my late 50s, I can see that most of the really significant things that have happened in my life have happened by accident.

This book is one of them.

There are only two ways to live your life. One: as though nothing is a miracle. The other: as though everything is.

Albert Einstein

2

You Are My Friends

In which I visit a mosque and 'go viral'

Often, we assume that to change the world we need to reach
a critical mass of power and influence. Certainly, some of the
great social changes that have happened in the last hundred
years – the civil rights movement, the end of apartheid, votes for
women – have happened because a lot of people came together.
But there is another way. Instead of critical mass John Paul
Lederach speaks about critical yeast. The principle of critical
yeast is that if you want to change the world you don't need a
big army but a few strategically connected people. Yeast makes
dough rise, not because there is a lot of it, but because small
amounts are mixed together, warmed and kneaded. It's not
wrong to want to change the world. In fact, if you don't want
to change it, you have probably dialled down your ambition
too far. But being overwhelmed by the task won't help anyone.
Instead, we need to recognize that change starts with small
actions – doing something when you could have done nothing.
Everyday Activism sometimes means acting on instinct. It can
mean doing something that feels a bit daft, just because it seems
like a good idea at the time. That could be a very big and sacri-
ficial thing, but it can equally be a really small and local thing.
In this case, a very trivial action that was only supposed to be
local ended up pitching me into an international spotlight.

I usually wake up to the *Today* programme on BBC Radio 4. On the morning of 15 March 2019 I woke up to the news of terrible events in Christchurch, New Zealand. A young man had walked into two mosques during Friday prayers. He was carrying five guns. He'd carefully decorated each one in Tippex with slogans and symbols representing white supremacy. He shot 51 people dead and wounded 49 others. Then he got in his car and set off for a third location. He was arrested before he got there.

Christchurch is known as a fairly tranquil city in a relatively peaceful country. It's about 12,000 miles from Manchester, where I live. I've never been there, and I don't suppose I ever will. But my first thought when I heard the bulletin was that if this could happen in Christchurch it could happen anywhere. I wondered how the people who gather for Friday prayers at my local mosque in Levenshulme might feel this morning. Angry? Mistrustful? Afraid? I couldn't stop thinking about them all morning.

At about half past eleven people would be leaving work and heading towards the mosque for Friday prayers. I thought I would walk there too. I wasn't quite sure why. I just felt I wanted to be with them. But as I was leaving the house I wondered what on earth I would do when I got there. I thought that I might look a bit silly just standing in the road and grinning. So I grabbed a piece of cardboard – an old file hanger – and wrote a message on it: *You are my friends. I will watch while you pray.* I read it back to myself. The idea of watching while someone else prayed sounded a bit creepy. I stuck a piece of paper over it, and tried again. *You are my friends. I will* keep *watch while you pray.* That was better. Then I set off.

When I got to the mosque people were starting to arrive. I stood outside with my sign. It's a big mosque with several hundred worshippers. I was struck by how much of a rush people were in as they arrived. Just like my own church, I thought, with people hurrying in during the first hymn. Some looked a bit wary when they saw me standing by the entrance. Perhaps they wondered if I was some kind of protester, or an evangelist hoping to convert them. When they saw the card, some of them smiled, but most just walked straight past me.

I stayed at the gate for about an hour and a half, until people started to leave. When the worshippers came out, everyone wanted to shake my hand, thank me, and share salaam with me. Someone even took a photo of me with my cardboard sign! It turned out that the Imam had seen me as he walked into the mosque and had mentioned me in his sermon. For a day that had started with such bleak news, it was a lovely atmosphere. A man outside the mosque was cooking chicken biryani, and he gave me a foil box full of it – so that felt like a win. Then I toddled off home to get on with my day.

The man who took the photo uploaded it to our community website, with a message saying, 'Who is this guy?' As the day went on I discovered that the picture was being shared widely on the internet, and not just on our local Facebook page. Not only in the UK either, but around the world. I started to get messages by email and Twitter from strangers. At first, I replied to each message as it came in. Then they started coming faster and faster. By the end of the afternoon they were coming so fast that I couldn't even keep up with reading them. Beside the personal messages, there were likes and retweets and Facebook posts – literally millions of them – all sharing the picture, the one on the front of this book. By teatime I was starting to realize that I'd gone – if not viral, then at least fungal. I didn't post anything on social media myself, though my daughter posted a nice message saying she was proud of me. In the next few hours my picture was retweeted with warm messages from the weirdest range of people, from Jada Pinkett Smith to Monica Lewinsky.

And the snowball kept rolling down the hill, faster and faster. Within a few hours I was getting messages from journalists and radio and TV stations in every country you can imagine – from

Turkey, Egypt and Bangladesh. Who was I? Why had I done this? Would I be prepared to give an interview? I had to decide quickly how I was going to respond. I thought the best thing was to roll with it. So I made a decision that I would say yes to everyone except Piers Morgan – and that's what I did. On Saturday I did interviews back to back – by phone, by Skype, in TV studios … When Saturday evening came I breathed a sigh of relief thinking it was over. But then Australia and New Zealand woke up and started getting in touch. The attacks were in New Zealand, and the attacker had come from Australia. Perhaps the greatest privilege of all was to speak to the people of Christchurch, New Zealand via their local TV and radio stations. I was able to say that we in Manchester know something of what they are feeling because we have had our own atrocities – but that we also know that friendship can overcome fear. On Monday I had a message of thanks from the Prime Minister of New Zealand, the wonderful Jacinda Ardern. The Secretary-General of the United Nations mentioned me in a speech about reconciliation, and so did a minister from the UK Foreign Office.

Over the next few days I received in excess of 50,000 individual messages. They came from almost every country in the world, from Hollywood to Hyderabad. The photo was copied tens of millions of times. In 24 hours, my Twitter followers went up from 3,000 to over 15,000. Usually I regret about one in three of my tweets, but I realized I would need to start being more careful what I said. I became the subject of sermons and school assemblies and radio phone-ins. The responses were overwhelmingly positive – although of course there were a few unpleasant ones. I was raised in the Scottish parliament as an example of the need for social media platforms to censor abusive messages – though to this day I haven't been able to find the abusive messages they were referring to. One or two people asked what exactly I was planning to do if a gunman had approached the mosque. To be honest, I hadn't really thought about that. Armed with a file hanger and a flat cap, I made a pretty inadequate vigilante. But the point was to be there, and everybody visiting the mosque seemed to understand that.

Among the negative messages, one common complaint was, 'Are you going to stand guard outside every mosque in the world then?' To which my answer was, 'No, I'll stand outside *my* local mosque and *you* stand outside yours.' Indeed, people from other cities around the world started to do just that. I was sent pictures of people standing outside mosques in their own cities, some of them with signs saying *You are my friends. I will keep watch while you pray.* One lovely couple in Reading had even written their sign on an old file hanger – as if that was a key part of the plot. Another common message in the negative pile was, 'You wouldn't find Muslims protecting churches if it was the other way round.' But in fact, the following month, when a church in Sri Lanka was attacked by a Muslim gunman, groups from mosques all around the world did just that, standing outside their local churches in solidarity.

My family will confirm that I was bemused by the whole experience. The whole thing was unplanned, unexpected and completely disproportionate. The simple message I had tried to pass on is that friendship overcomes fear. Hatred doesn't generate itself. It is a by-product of fear; fear of someone who is just slightly different from me.

Some of the stuff that happened was a bit bizarre. A woman from Essex knitted a puppet of me holding my sign. An artist in Dorset painted me in oils. A man in New Zealand drew a cartoon picture of me on the side of a paper cup. I got some lovely offers too. The picture was particularly big in Turkey, apparently, and a generous guy there offered to ship me over there, so he could buy me a drink. A Muslim dentist in the Midlands wrote to say that in gratitude for my actions he would like to offer to whiten my teeth for free – which is a pretty back-handed compliment, really. I'm still reflecting on what has happened, and is continuing to happen. I wasn't expecting to be interviewed on *Voice of Islam* radio or bad-mouthed by Far Right groups or discussed on *Loose Women*. I am aware that all the nice things that were said to and about me (and all the not so nice things) were not actually being addressed to me personally, but to the action, and what it symbolized.

One of the themes to emerge from the tens of thousands of messages I have received is that Muslims in the UK and elsewhere live with a mild but perpetual undercurrent of threat. It is like a buzzing in the ears, varying in intensity according to context, but requiring constant vigilance. Of course, others also live with similar kinds of anxiety. Perhaps we all do, though as a white middle-class man in the UK my threat level is almost inaudible. For others it is like the relentless hum of tinnitus. Unwittingly, my tiny action and the message on my card seem to have suggested to people that I understood the impact of this level of persistent fear. The word 'Islamophobia' suggests a fear *of* Muslims, but the effect is to generate a fear *in* Muslims. Both sides of this unholy equation need to be dealt with.

I'm learning about the extraordinary power of symbol in everyday activism. The thing that 'went viral' was not me, but an image of a smiling bloke in a flat hat carrying a scrappy piece of cardboard with a message on. It's not even clear from the picture that I'm standing in front of a mosque, as the building was being redeveloped, and was surrounded by blue hoardings. That image is associated with an action. The particular action was as simple as standing on a pavement for 90 minutes, but the location, outside Medina Mosque in South Manchester, has proven to have a symbolic power vastly beyond anything I intended or could have planned. All I was doing was standing in a place where I don't immediately belong – outside the gate of a mosque complex. The fact of doing so was simple to the point of being trivial. But the meanings attached to the symbol seem to have had a powerful resonance. I can't sum up those meanings adequately in words. A symbol goes beyond words, and its meaning belongs to the person who reads it more than the person who inscribes it. It was a completely naive thing to do, and that was where its power lay. If I'd tried to manufacture it, it would have failed.

Subsequently, as the image of my symbolic action began to go viral, I realized that I had an opportunity to reinforce it with a few words. This is the function of the hashtag on a tweet, or the tag on an image. The words I settled on were #Friendship NotFear. I've attached them to every tweet and used them in every interview. There's no automatic connection between the words and the image, any more than there is a connection between the Nike swoosh and the words 'Just do it'. They were my attempt to cash out the symbol, and give people some way to verbalize their identification with it. It couldn't have happened the other way around. The symbol is primary and the words secondary.

What people seemed to respond to was an image of an ordinary-looking bloke, wearing a flat cap and a jumper, doing something a bit transgressive. I had jumped over the fence and gone onto a neighbour's territory. That was exactly what the Christchurch gunman had done, except that where he went with guns and hatred, I went open-handed and smiling. Some people thanked me for taking a risk. What risk? A small risk of rejection, perhaps. The possibility of being misunderstood. But you can't start a friendship of any kind without taking small risks.

If I had had any idea when I woke up that morning that my picture was going to be shared around the world, I would at least have brushed my hair. It's nice when someone sends you a message saying, 'You are a symbol of the world I want to live in.' It's nice when someone shouts 'hero' at you in the street, or stops you in Asda and asks for a selfie. Nice nice, but also weird nice. I am just trying to roll with it. Tomorrow it will all be forgotten. Probably.

The growing good of the world is partly dependent on unhistoric acts; and that things are not so ill with you and me as they might have been, is half owing to the number who lived faithfully a hidden life, and rest in unvisited tombs.

George Eliot, Middlemarch

3

The Painful Truth

*In which I have an awkward encounter
with my neighbours*

Every year the compilers of the Oxford English Dictionary
*pick a Word of the Year. They choose a word that has taken
root in our vocabulary in the previous 12 months, and that
sums up something about the times we're living in. The Word
of the Year for 2016 was 'post-truth'.*

*'Post-truth' means that objective facts are less influential in
shaping public opinion than appeals to emotion and personal
beliefs. It's a way of describing a world where some advertisers
and politicians and journalists are quite happy to say anything
– not because it relates to the way the world actually is, but
because it will win them the customers or voters or readers they
want to attract.*

*The trouble is, if we settle for anything less than the truth, we
quickly reach a point where we can't trust anyone at all. We're
all learning to read our emails with a degree of scepticism in
case we're being scammed. We've taught ourselves to assume
that politicians are not to be trusted because we believe they
are always on the make. In a post-truth world we all become
cynical – suspicious of our leaders and suspicious of our neighbours. Never mind the rate of the pound against the dollar
– truth is by far the most valuable currency we have. Sometimes, just telling the truth, where a lie would be easier, is an
act of rebellion.*

A while ago I came across a very unusual and impressive man. He runs a small private chain of estate agents in the south-east of England. What's unusual about that? Well, at the risk of getting myself into trouble, he's unusual among estate agents because he and his colleagues have adopted a policy of always telling the truth.

I asked him how this rather remarkable state of affairs came about. He told me that he was working with his partners to draw up a set of core values they could use to advertise their firm. When someone suggested they should put 'honesty' on the list they realized that they could not, in all honesty, do so. They agreed that in a hundred tiny ways they lied to them-selves and their customers every day – exaggerating the size of properties, or the degree of interest they'd had from buyers and so on. And they felt uncomfortable with it. They felt that their firm had become infected with a culture of untruth. They even told lies about why they were late for meetings with clients, when it would have been just as easy to tell the truth. So they took a decision – I shall get in trouble for saying this, but it may even be unique – that they would always tell the truth.

Now no one would suggest that lying (by estate agents or anyone else) is a recent invention. But I have a suspicion that something significant has happened over recent years. We've learnt to live in a culture of lies, hype and spin. If a recent study in California is to be believed, people lie up to 20 times a day. The researchers suggested that the West is suffering from an epidemic of untruth.

I like to think I always tell the truth – but I was sorely tempted recently. We'd just moved into a new area, and to be honest it was a bit more up-market than we were used to, so we were keen to make a good impression on the neighbours.

On our very first day in the new house, we tried to keep the dog indoors to give her time to get used to her new home, but what with all the moving boxes in and out through the front door, somehow she got out. At about half past eleven in the morning I heard a scratching sound at the front door. I went to open it – and found our dog proudly wagging her tail. At her feet was the neighbours' pet rabbit, stone dead.

Well, what would you have done? I seriously considered just moving back out there and then and leaving no forwarding address. Then I thought perhaps I could get another rabbit and sneak it into the next-door hutch. I even thought I might sling the dead rabbit back over the neighbours' fence and pretend it had died of a heart attack. All of these seemed easier – kinder even – than telling the truth. But that's what I did. It's quite possibly the hardest sentence I've ever uttered. 'Hello. I'm your new neighbour ... and this in the cardboard box, this is your dead rabbit.'

It took a bit of forgiving, but eventually we became quite good friends. At least I didn't have to keep up a lie for weeks and months. It was Mark Twain who said, 'If you tell the truth, you don't have to remember anything.' And that seems to me important.

Some people struggle to tell the truth without applying a coat of varnish. Politicians spin, accountants are 'creative' and the best of us may be tempted to throw the odd 'sickie' during the World Cup. Maybe it seems like that doesn't matter. But even a thin layer of gloss, if you apply it often enough, eats into your soul like – like whatever that stuff is that eats into your teeth if you have too much sugar in your tea. Lack of truth leads to lack of trust; lack of trust leads to scarred relation-ships; scarred relationships eat up the time and energy that should be spent on living and loving.

Does all this really matter? I think it does. If you're going to trust me for the truth, you will need to know that I haven't distorted it, exaggerated it, changed or embellished it, but told it like it is.

Laughter is carbonated holiness.

Anne Lamott

4

I Wonder ...

In which a group of adults behave like children

There's an infectious cynicism in our culture that means we often expect the worst and struggle to believe in goodness. It's at the root of a lot of contemporary comedy. We snigger at the possibility that a politician might tell the truth. We scoff at the idea that a story might end well. When we're presented with possibilities beyond our own imagination, we're inclined to laugh in disbelief. We're sceptical because we find it hard to envision a future outside the limitations of our own expectations. It's a struggle to stay open to future possibilities that might amaze me. It seems to me that one of the most revolutionary acts we can make in the twenty-first century is to not give up hope.

A group of scientists recently announced that they had discovered a new shade of the colour black. Apparently, it's 25 times blacker than the blackest black anyone's ever made before. I suppose you can't exactly say they've *discovered* a new shade of black. Presumably it was there before they managed to measure it or recreate it. But it's kind of exciting because it means the whole spectrum of colours has grown a bit. In a way it's a bit like discovering a whole new continent that we didn't know was there.

I was delighted that the scientist who developed this new black was called Dr Richard Brown. He was very excited about it. 'It's incredibly beautiful,' he said, 'like black velvet.'

The only trouble is, you need scientific instruments to tell just how black it is. To you and me, black is just – well, black. But there's obviously much more to black than meets the eye.

All my life I've been blissfully unaware of how much detail and richness there is, even in the simple colour black. I guess quite often I just look at the surface of things. I'm rather ashamed to have missed so much of the intensity of the world. Evidently there's a whole range of detail that I'm just not equipped to pick up. It makes me wonder what else I've been missing. Is there a mass of sounds that my ears just aren't hearing? Are there a million different flavours that my taste-buds have been ignoring? The mind boggles.

If you believe in God, then this extravagance will make you stand back in awe. God's attention to detail – amazing. Fancy creating stuff that's far cleverer than we're even equipped to experience. And if you don't believe in God, well, maybe the world's just a more wonderful place than we'd realized till now.

A little while ago I spent a week on a camping holiday with a gathering of families from housing estates all over the country. All of us came from difficult areas, and most had very real experience of poverty. We were all pretty stressed out when we arrived. In a far corner of the campsite there was a huge yellow bouncy castle – the biggest I've ever seen. The children were wide-eyed when they first saw it, and they played on it for hour after hour, day after day. It's just amazing how long they can keep going on those things.

After a few days it was obvious that one or two of the adults were eyeing this castle up too. It looked such fun. So, one night, after dark, when we felt sure the kids were asleep, we drove a couple of cars down the field and shone their head-lights onto the bouncy castle. Then under the stars the grown-ups took their shoes off and jumped on the castle. We bounced and giggled and pushed each other over until late into the night, and we were all out of breath and couldn't stand up for laughing. It was fantastic. It was like we had discovered something innocent in ourselves that adulthood had almost completely obscured. I'm sure the adults on the bouncy castle behaved worse than the children, but that was because it had been so long since most of us had connected with that part of ourselves that sparkled and wondered. The amazing thing was that, even for those whose everyday lives were grindingly tough, the sense of joy was still available. You just had to mine for it, and not give up until you had found it.

A little while later, some friends and I decided to climb Mount Snowdon. It was a lovely sunny day and as we climbed the Pig Track we were getting spectacular views across the landscape below.

At one point we walked past a big glacial lake. At the side of the lake was another party of walkers. They were all standing in the shallows at the water's edge, gazing intently downwards. We stopped and asked them what they were doing. They told us they had been skimming stones across the surface of the lake when one of the women had accidentally skimmed her wedding ring straight off her finger and into the water. They'd all been standing there for an hour or more, looking for it. We joined them in the hunt.

The water was crystal clear, and the bottom of the lake was covered in smooth round golden pebbles. The bright sunshine was playing cruel tricks on them, making little gold circles dance all over the surface of the water. Every so often one of them would bend down into the lake and make a grab for what they thought was the ring. But it wasn't. They were all ready to give up. All except for the woman whose ring it was. For her it was priceless – irreplaceable. She'd have stayed all day and turned over every pebble in the lake to find it.

Anyway, there we were on that mountain in Wales when suddenly one of my friends standing on a rock in the shallows shot his hand down in the water and held the ring up high. A cheer went up that must have been heard all over Wales. We'd only met each other a few minutes before, but now we were hugging each other and dancing together in the freezing water. A party broke out. The other walkers making their way up the hillside must have thought we'd gone bananas.

I guess there are some things that children have access to that grown-ups usually don't: a lack of inhibitions; the energy to bounce till you're out of breath; a sense of wonder perhaps, instead of the cynicism of adulthood; a powerful combination of natural justice together with the faith that things can be different, and an ability to play too. I need to recover that on a regular basis, or else paying the mortgage and catching the train to work and all those other grown-up things knock all the bounce out of me. So sometimes I wait till no one's looking, then run down the road as fast as I can till I'm out of breath and can't run any longer. Sometimes I lock myself in the car and drive down the motorway with the radio on disgracefully loud and sing along at the top of my voice. Occasionally I buy a big bar of chocolate and eat it all myself, celebrating the wonder of creation. I like to do at least one thing each day that reconnects me with full-on, hair-down, childish joy. I find it's just as effective as ten minutes praying or a couple of hours' worrying any day. Adult life is a bruising thing, but this life is intended for joy.

Hope is not to be confused with optimism. Hope believes despite the evidence and then works to see the evidence change.

Desmond Tutu

5

The Battle of Adswood Library

In which a community borrows its own library

Part of the role of the Everyday Activist is to choose to stand alongside people who have little power and stand up to the over-mighty. That's easier said than done, but I have come to understand that one of the things that works most powerfully is poking fun.

When a cartoonist draws a picture of a politician with their trousers down they are using the power of the pen to redress the imbalance between us and our leaders. At best, that's the role of satire – though it can easily become self-serving. Edward Lewis called laughter 'the sensual pleasure of democracy' because of its levelling effect. Pricking the bubbles of the pompous may be satisfying, but if that's the end of the story nothing much has been achieved. Comedians may bring down the over-mighty, but they're not always great at building up again. That's the role of the rest of us. A joke, provided it is outrageous enough, can be a sign of hope, because it says that the way things are is not the way things have to be. In the space created by laughter we see the possibility of a renewed, just world.

The relationships we made in the 12 years our family spent living in Adswood were among the most formative of our lives. There are so many stories I could tell you about it. Here's one.

Throughout the 1990s and beyond I lived with my family on a downtown housing estate called Adswood, in South Manchester. Adswood wasn't one of those huge estates that get a lot of attention. To be honest it hadn't got much going for it. It was just an island of deprivation in the sea of mediocrity that is Stockport. But the friends and neighbours I met in Adswood were beautiful people, and they have left a mark on me, more than anyone I've ever met.

I stood out like a sore thumb in Adswood. I was working at the BBC at the time, and every day I would go out in the morning and come back onto the estate at night carrying my massively untrendy briefcase. I learnt that some of the children assumed I was a doctor. It was a fair assumption, since no professional people actually lived on the estate – no teachers, no social workers, not even the vicar, who had a large detached house a couple of miles away. Adswood was a rough and ready place to live. We saw many people move onto the estate and move straight off again. When we first moved there, one of the local councillors said to us, 'The trouble with Adswood is, it doesn't have a voice.'

The one thing Adswood did have was a library. I say a library – it was just a single room with bookshelves and a friendly librarian. Older people from the estate would meet there for coffee during the day, and kids who lived in over-crowded houses went there after school to do their homework and get help from the friendly librarian.

Then the local council decided that Adswood library needed to close. Nothing spiteful – just the usual cost-cutting exercise in the town hall. Who needs a library in a place where people don't even have books in their homes?

When the news filtered through, most of the residents just accepted it as inevitable. One of the strategies many Adswood people used to get through life was simply not to entertain hope. If you don't hope for things to be better, you don't get hurt when they turn out worse. The politicians knew this, and it made Adswood an easy target. Still, for a few people, the loss of Adswood library was too much to take. They wanted to fight for it. Soon a little protest group formed. 'We've got to keep the library open. What can we do to make the council change its mind?'

Some people wanted to chain themselves to the railings or lie down in front of the bull-dozers. But we were afraid people would just say, 'Well what can you expect from Adswood people?' We knew that the Battle for Adswood Library was a battle we were most likely to lose – so we decided that whatever we did needed to be fun. We chose our weapons carefully – laughter, mockery, mischief.

First, we had to get noticed. So we invited children's authors to visit Adswood library to give book readings. Amazingly, some really high-profile people came, and the local paper, which had only come to Adswood for stories about drugs and crime before, was delighted to print pictures of happy children in a packed library. Still we needed to up our game. We needed to get Adswood library onto the front page. So we wrote to the authors of the most borrowed books, and told them what was about to happen to the library. Without exception they wrote supportive letters back. Jilly Cooper and Spike Milligan, Jeffrey Archer and Alan Bennett; they all signed up for the Battle for Adswood Library. Roger McGough even wrote a poem: The Ballad of Adswood Library. Their letters took us to a new level of publicity. But the more we embarrassed them, the more the council dug their heels in. The leader of the council went on national radio and gave a massively patronising interview. 'These people in Adswood have no understanding of money,' he said. 'They just don't know how difficult it is for councillors to juggle the books.'

So the next week we hired a juggler. We invited all the local councillors to come to Adswood library for a lesson. They didn't come of course, but the next week the front page of the *Stockport Express* was a full-page picture of Adswood library, with a man in a clown costume teaching a group of children how to juggle books. The councillors were not impressed. The council leader came to my house at night to persuade us to back off. Stockport Council's struggle to close the library was being noticed elsewhere, she said. They were becoming a laughing stock. She even offered my wife a seat on the council if we would give up the Battle for Adswood Library. We didn't. Membership of the library was growing. It was now the busiest library in Stockport. Pretty much everyone on the estate had a ticket. And that gave us an idea.

One cold morning in October, when the librarian arrived to open the library, she found a huge queue outside. The whole estate had descended on the little library with their tickets. Now in our area you could borrow up to ten books on one ticket. If you are a single parent with three children, that's 40 books, which is virtually a shelf-full. And there were scores of us. Mums were coming in with buggies and going away loaded up with books. The local vicar turned up to lend support, and went away with ten Jackie Collins novels. I picked out ten Judith Krantz novels, mainly because they were good and thick – almost two feet of solid books on one ticket.

As battles go, this was fun. There was a party atmosphere. The librarian was delighted to be so busy. The council couldn't really object, because after all, we were only doing exactly what you are supposed to do with a library – borrowing the books – only we borrowed them all at once. Every single one of them. By the end of the morning, the library shelves were empty. It was a celebration – of books, of community, of the fact that we were just plain right to want our library kept open. We made sure that TV cameras were there to record it. The next day we were on the front page of most of the national newspapers as The Community that Borrowed its Library.

The councillors were furious. They set a date for the library to close. It looked as if we had lost The Battle for Adswood Library.

The night before the day that the library was due to close, we broke the law for the first and only time. After dark we broke into the building. To be honest, breaking and entering was a local skill that we had probably under-used in the campaign thus far. We went to the inner door that led to the library and squirted a tube of superglue into the lock. Then we changed the screws on the handle for clutch screws, so it couldn't be removed.

In the morning, when the librarian arrived at 8.30 to open the library for the last time, she couldn't get in. She called her bosses, who called a locksmith, who came and opened the library. The council sent two big security guards to the building to make sure it stayed open. When the press and TV cameras arrived, we were able to point out that the council that thought it was so important to keep the library open today, were going to close it for good tomorrow.

Still, the Battle for Adswood Library was lost. But we had won some significant victories. Now, when the councillors said, 'The trouble with Adswood is, it doesn't have a voice,' we were able to say, 'The trouble with Adswood is, no one's listening.'

There is a postscript to this story.

Just a few yards from the library there was a roundabout with a road junction where young children used to cross the road to get to school. Cars would come round the corner at speed, and there had been several nasty accidents or near misses. Residents persuaded the council that they should install a pelican crossing – a pedestrian crossing controlled by traffic lights. They duly installed the traffic lights and painted the lines on the road, but due to a dispute between the council and the electricity board they never actually switched on the lights to control the crossing. Consequently, the crossing was more rather than less dangerous than it had been before.

One morning, just after school drop-off time, parents and babies from the estate gathered at the crossing with their buggies and trollies. At a given signal they all walked into the road, and stopped half-way, making the road completely impassable. Traffic started backing up in both directions, with angry drivers hooting their horns. After a few minutes, the queue was the best part of a mile long. Then the police arrived. We explained why we were protesting. They were very polite and sympathetic, but they said that if we didn't leave the crossing they would have to start making arrests. We agreed to go, but we had another plan up our sleeves. We had asked each child to bring a favourite soft toy to the protest with them. As we walked off the road, each child left a teddy or a cuddly toy behind; a furry road-block, a picket line of cuddly animals where the crossing should have been. We stood at the side of the road, but the traffic wouldn't move. No one wanted to be the first to drive over the teddies. We took photos of course, and sent them to the press. They loved it. The council hated it.

I wish I could say that no cuddly toys were harmed in the protest, but I can't. In truth, they all survived unscathed except one – a multi-coloured dinosaur called Daisy. Sadly, she was caught under the wheels of a 310 bus and lost an eye. Still, she bore her injury with pride, and was forever after lauded in the community as a hero.

But the mighty councillors of Stockport had learnt their lesson. They didn't want another Adswood Library on their hands. The next morning the traffic lights were connected, and the crossing was safe. Adswood had found a voice.

Mostly we have just enough light to see the next step: what we have to do in the coming hour, or the following day. The art of living is to enjoy what we can see and not complain about what remains in the dark. When we are able to take the next step with the trust that we will have enough light ... we can walk through life with joy and be surprised at how far we go.

Henri Nouwen

6

A Load of Rubbish

In which I accidentally break the law twice ...
or possibly three times

*When it comes to changing the world, a certain amount of
strategy is needed. Many changes that we might want to see
are unachievable in the short term. But that doesn't mean we
can't do anything. Everyday Activists put up signposts. By that
I mean that we take actions that point the way to a different
reality. A signpost is an acted parable. It may simply be a way
to help expand people's minds, by saying, 'What if the world
was like this?' Signposts have to stand out, so they are usually
visual and often unusual. A really powerful, prophetic picture
is a perfect microcosm of the truth it is pointing to. Bread and
wine; teddies and toddlers; borrowing the books. It is a taster
that makes people feel hungry for a new reality.*

*Signposts may be quite small actions – an open door, a smile
to a stranger, a gift of food; or they can be quite big actions, like
helping a whole community to come together and clean away
their rubbish. But before I tell you about that, let me tell you
about Jason.*

I've already said that the Adswood estate in the 1990s was
a rough and ready place to live. It was so different from the
ordered middle-class suburbs that we'd grown up in that at
first Jane and I understood almost nothing about how to live
well there. It was sheer naivety that got us through our first six

months living in Adswood ... plus a minibus. One of the biggest poverties on an estate like Adswood is transport. We needed a vehicle to visit our families in other parts of the country, but we realized that owning a 'family' car would benefit mostly ourselves, so we opted for a more flexible vehicle: a battered old crew bus, with wooden seats down each side. It was dual-purpose, in that you could fill it full of young people for a trip to the seaside, or you could load it up with second-hand furniture that someone wanted shifted. Very few people on the estate owned cars, but everybody knew we had a bus, and that we were sometimes willing to drive people or stuff around in it. For that reason, if nothing else, these quirky southern incomers were useful, and worth protecting.

Adswood used to get even more rough and ready when Jason was out of prison. Jason was in his late 20s and lived in the house across the green from us. He was a big bloke, and lots of people on the estate were quite scared of him, or at least felt they needed to keep on the right side of him. In my innocence I wanted to get to know the human behind the tattoos, so I looked for an opportunity to spend some 'quality time' with Jason.

My opportunity came one autumn evening, as I was parking our van on the drive. Jason strolled up the pavement and said hello. It was the first time we had ever spoken. 'Hi, Jason,' I said. 'I haven't seen you around for a while.' As soon as the words came out of my mouth it occurred to me that that's not the most polite greeting for a serial convict. He laughed it off. He'd been wondering, he said, if I could give him some help. 'Of course,' I said. Jason said that he was helping a friend of his with a building project, and he needed to move some timber from his house to his mate's house on the other side of the estate. He'd been eyeing up my minibus, and wondered if I could help him move the stuff. 'Jump in,' I said, delighted at this opportunity to play the Good Samaritan. Jason got into the front seat beside me and I drove the bus around the green to his place, parking it up with the back doors facing his house. I offered to help him load the wood into the van. 'No, mate,' he said. 'You wait here.' So I sat in the driver's seat and watched as he disappeared down the side passage of his house to collect the wood. He was gone a long time, but eventually he came back with a mate, and four long pieces of construction grade timber slung over their shoulders. I nodded at Jason's friend as they slid the wood into the back of the van, then went back for more. A few minutes later they were back again with a similar load ... and then another, and another. They were obviously working on quite a substantial job.

After about three-quarters of an hour of heavy lifting, the van was about half full with beams, planks and floorboards, but still they kept coming. As I waited for the next batch to arrive with my new friends I started to doubt myself. I wondered quite how they had stored such a large quantity of wood in one small council house. Then it occurred to me. Jason's house backed on to the railway line. And on the other side of the railway line was a builder's merchant. A builder's merchant that supplied builders. With wood. Wood that Jason and his mate were meticulously lifting across the railway line and loading into the back of my little white minibus.

'I reckon that's as much as we can get in,' said Jason. 'We'll have to make a second trip.'

'Jason, are you sure this is all your wood?' I asked. He looked at me quizzically. I realized that he wasn't answering my question. What his quizzical look was saying was 'What exactly are you going to do about it?'

I drove the van to Jason's friend's house and waited while they unloaded it. Then as they were taking the last batch of planks out of my van and into their new home, I quickly shut the back doors and drove away. What else was I to do? I saw Jason many times after that of course, but we never mentioned his building project.

Another time I was sitting in my front room when I heard

someone outside trying and trying to get their car started. It was a cold, wet winter's night, so I thought I'd do the neighbourly thing and give them a hand. Sure enough, when I went out there were two youngish guys pushing the car, while Jason sat in the front seat trying to bump start it. I said hello, got behind the car and started to help push it.

It was only after another couple of unsuccessful attempts to get it moving that a thought occurred to me. I know why you can't get this car to start. It's because you haven't got the key. And you haven't got the key because it's not your car. I'm helping you to hot-wire a nicked car. That was when I realized that the other guys were wearing black woolly hats and gloves … whilst I'd left my crystal-clear paw-prints all over the grubby back windscreen.

One of the problems caused by the lack of available transport was getting rid of rubbish. Just behind the builders' yard was a council tip (or Eco-Centre as it was optimistically named). Even though the local tip was less than half a mile away, it was too far to carry a worn-out sofa or a fridge that had broken down. Even with our van, we couldn't shift everybody's old stuff, so very often things like furniture or white goods just got left in front gardens or dumped in the street. Living in sight of a refuse dump but not being able to get rid of your own waste is one of the indignities that Adswood people shared with people in poverty all over the world.

At one stage the build-up of unwanted stuff in the streets and gardens was getting really bad. Then a little group of residents had an idea. They decided to hold a clean-up weekend. The local builders' yard generously lent us a flat-bed truck, and we toured the estate one Saturday picking up all the junk we could find. Lots of people came out to help. After all, no one *wants* to live in a rubbish heap. Pretty soon the lorry was full, and we took it off to the local tip to empty it.

There was a barrier at the entrance to the tip, manned by a bloke in a high-vis jacket. As we drove up to the barrier he waved us to stop. 'Sorry, mate,' he said. 'You can't bring that in here.'

'Why not?' we asked.

'We only take domestic waste. No commercial vehicles.'

'But this *is* domestic waste,' I protested. And I explained what we had been doing. 'Sorry,' he said. 'No trucks, no lorries, no exceptions.' My heart sank. I weighed up the possibility of taking a run-up and crashing the van through the barrier James Bond style, but my inner Daniel Craig was AWOL. The weekend clean-up had seemed like such a simple idea, but now we were defeated at the last hurdle. There was no way this guy was going to lift the barrier. It looked as if we might have to drive back round the estate giving everyone their rubbish back.

At that point the six Adswood women who had come with me to the tip got out of the truck. They stood in a line facing the guy in the yellow jacket, leaning on their brooms and shovels. They were scary. Women you wouldn't mess with; grannies and mums and aunties who had brought up kids on Adswood, built lives together with almost no resources, and seen off men far bigger than this guy with his clipboard and his orders from the council. They were women who were not planning to take 'no' for an answer. The wonderful thing was that not a word was spoken. They simply stared at him, and he looked back at them, and then he pushed the lever to open the barrier and I drove the truck through into the tip. Then the women hopped on the back and worked together to unload it into the concrete hoppers. This was girl power the Spice Girls could only ever dream of.

When we had emptied the lorry we drove back to the estate, waving cheery smiles to the security guard as we passed on our way out. Then we went back for more.

By this time, word had spread around the estate. House by house, people came out and stopped the lorry. They were catching the vision of a clear-out. Neighbours worked together to shift stuff from their gardens, or invited each other in to help clean out their houses. Sometimes people had whole rooms full of rubbish they just hadn't been able to shift. The houses are quite small, but they'd been living with it because they couldn't see a way to get rid of it. The rubbish had just become part of the furniture. And now their own neighbours were helping them to shift it.

We worked all day. Altogether the lorry went back and forth to the tip seven times. Each time we waved cheerily to the man on the gate. By the third time he had been joined by other council workers. Their orders had changed, and now they formed a high-vis guard of honour as the piled-up van drove into the Eco-Centre. It was an exciting, liberating, joyful day. For some families it was a real turning point – a new start. More space, getting rid of a lot of unwanted stuff. Same people, same estate, same old house, but a freedom to have another go; to start again.

Be kind whenever possible. It is always possible.

Dalai Lama

7

Rocky's Story

In which I meet a group of strangers,
and behave really badly

One of the most significant decisions we can make is where we
will live. I suspect that most of us either don't think about it
too much, or if we do, we choose to live somewhere that feels
comfortable and safe – where the other people are like us. But
life is an adventure, and you can't easily have an adventure in
a place where you feel safe. As an Everyday Activist I decided
early on that I want to live amongst people who are not like
me. I want to escape the echo chamber. I want to buy my food
from shops that sell stuff I don't recognize. I want to read
newspapers with views I don't agree with, and hang out with
people who challenge me, and make me feel uncomfortable
and even a bit scared.

This takes a bit of humility. European missionaries and
entrepreneurs have a terrible history of marching into places
where we didn't belong and imposing our culture on other
people. If we go to places where we don't belong, we do it on
the condition that we are not there to change anyone, but to
share and learn with them. And that poses a further challenge.
If I, a Croydon boy, live in, say, County Durham, should I try
to adopt a Geordie accent? Absolutely not. The challenge is to
be myself, and allow other people to be themselves, and take
joy in what we have in common, and in our differences too.

In my late 20s I lived in north-east England in an ex-pit village called Pelton Fell, just outside the market town of Chester-le-Street, or *Chessleestree*, as it is correctly pronounced. We lived in a cute little semi-detached house, sandwiched between the general store and the chip shop, so the street outside our house was a natural gathering place for teenagers who had nothing to do. Between our front window and the road was a paved square about 15 feet wide, surrounded by a waist high brick wall. It made an ideal wrestling ring. Night after night groups of mean-looking kids would sit on the brick wall in front of our house and make up games that usually involved kicking the hell out of each other. They were aged between about 11 and 15, and to my public school mind they looked like extras from the cast of *Oliver*. The house was so tiny that if I was sitting in the front room they were almost within arm's length. This didn't use to happen in suburban Croydon, where I grew up. In Croydon you could die in your front room and the smell wouldn't reach the road for a week. But in Pelton Fell, everybody quite literally knew who you were with, what you were watching on TV and what you were talking about. I could hear every word they said too, though as a south London boy deep in Geordie territory I didn't even understand a tenth of it. I did catch that one of them was called Rocky – though I doubt that was the name he'd been christened with. To leave my house I had to walk through a crowd of young people hanging out in my own front yard. I would steel myself and walk purposefully out each day, weaving between Rocky and his mates, with a forced smile and a cheery greeting. They were rough tough kids, and the honest truth is, I was afraid of them.

I had been hired by a local church to be a youth worker. I could not have been less prepared for the job. There was a gulf like the Grand Canyon between me and the kids sitting on my wall, and I had no idea how to cross it. But I took a principled decision that I should try to engage with these guys. I certainly wasn't going to start our relationship by trying to throw them out of my front yard. They needed to know that I was friendly. I would show them the love of Jesus, in sign language if necessary.

One evening I was sitting in my front room writing a story at a typewriter. (Already I realize that that is about the most middle-class sentence ever written.) The net curtains meant that during the day I could see out, but I couldn't be seen. I was so engrossed in my work that I didn't notice it getting dark outside, so that I could no longer see out of the window but I and my brightly lit desk were perfectly visible to the outside world. Suddenly my writing was interrupted by the *plink* of a stone hitting the window – followed by deep pubertal laughter. I jumped out of my skin. The boys had clearly seen me and were sending me a message. I went to the window and looked out, but I couldn't see anyone. I drew the curtains and went back to my work. Then, a minute later ... *plink*. Another stone, and another throaty laugh from the kids. Easy Tiger, I thought. They are just kids. Don't overreact. You need to show them the love of God. *Plink, plink*. Two more stones, and even louder laughter.

Acting on pure instinct, I leapt up out of my chair and ran to the front door. Red in the face I threw it open and bawled at them at the top of my voice. 'What the $*&%£@ are you doing? Get the @%*&$ out of my front yard. Leave me alone you little £%$*&s or I'll call the police.' But I was shouting at their backs as they ran up the road, laughing. They had got exactly the reaction they had been hoping for.

I, on the other hand, turned back into the house feeling like Judas Iscariot's less successful younger brother. In one 20-second burst of anger I had negated everything I had gone to the north-east of England for. More particularly I had given away who I truly was, instead of the plaster face I'd wanted to show them. I was a complete failure. I was ready to hand in my youth work card and head back to Croydon to retrain as a bus driver. I sat on the bottom of the stairs with my head in my hands.

About two minutes later there was a timid knock at the front door. I looked up to see that in my anger I had left it slightly open. A cold north-east fog was seeping into the house. I went over and opened the door a couple of inches further. It was Rocky. He was grinning. 'Got a light?' he said. Rocky was about 12. 'I'll go and get one,' I said. I'd never owned a cigarette lighter in my life, but I went into the kitchen and found the box of matches we used to light the cooker. I took them back to him. The whole gang of boys had now lined up behind Rocky – about half a dozen of them. 'Got a brew?' 'Yes,' I said – and without waiting, they pushed past me and made their way into the front room, which moments earlier had been my private, protected space. Four of them crammed themselves on our new two-seater sofa and two of them perched on the back with their wet trainers dangling on the fabric. I would never have dared to do that.

For the next three years our house was rarely without a group of young people in it. Whenever a light was on they were drawn to the house like moths to a flame. They hung out, taught me about their lives, ate crisps and fought on the sofa. I learnt to love the smell of teenager mixed with cigarette smoke and honesty. They made me into a youth worker and showed me the love of Jesus. God knows what I showed them.

Courage calls to courage everywhere.

Millicent Fawcett

8

Time-wasting

In which my teenage son teaches me an important lesson

I once went on a course about time management. I was reluctant to go, because I thought it would be a waste of time. In fact, I learnt some helpful things about the way I organize my days. I discovered that I have a strong tendency to put off tasks that I think are going to be difficult or unpleasant. That's not rocket science, I suppose. Whenever there's an uncomfortable phone call to be made, or a boring job to be done, things like ironing or loading the dishwasher suddenly become unusually attractive. Time management taught me how to separate what's urgent from what's important; how to move at walking pace instead of running; how to balance mundane tasks with things that will make a real difference.

What they didn't mention on my time management course was the glorious business of wasting time. In a world that is driven by achievement, status and productivity, wasting time can be an act of rebellion. I only discovered well into my long period of unemployment that I had been given the precious gift of availability. So many people I know are gifted, insightful and passionate but completely unavailable. Availability has taken me to some of the most interesting places in my life. And it turns out that availability is one of the first preconditions for Everyday Activism.

I am sitting in the car outside Kwiksave. It's half past nine at night and all the shops are shut. It's cold, and I'm just sitting here alone in the furthest corner of a huge empty car park. What a waste of time!

In the middle distance at the far end of the car park is a lanky teenager. He's wearing a hoody and baggy jeans that start half-way down his bum and finish about six inches after his legs do. He has a woolly hat like a tea-cosy pulled right down over his head. And he's riding backwards and forwards, backwards and forwards on his skateboard ... his Christmas skateboard that we picked so carefully from the catalogue, poring over the pictures till we found the one with just the right wheels, the right bearings, the right trucks, the right deck. I learnt a whole new vocabulary and I have nowhere else to use it. What a waste of time!

Every day I try to talk to him. I ask him how school has been. 'Good,' he mumbles. I ask him if he has any plans for the evening. 'Maybe,' he grunts. I ask him what he thinks of Manchester United's season so far. He shrugs and says nothing. It's a waste of time.

I bring him down here to the car park some evenings, and I sit where I can see him in the distance. It's a deal we have. He wants some space to skateboard. I know it's not safe for a 14-year-old boy to be out after dark around here. In exchange for giving him a lift I'm allowed to keep an eye on him from a distance. So I sit here. What a waste of time!

I could be at home working. I could be reading a book. I could be surfing the internet for a better car insurance deal. I could be painting the bathroom ceiling. I could be watching television. But I'm sitting in an empty car park watching my son. Wasting my time.

If you watch him for a while you can see him learning. He's trying to 'ollie'. That means he rides up the car park, then kicks the back of the board so it lifts into the air and lands on the kerb, and he lands on top of it. It's quite a skill. I've watched him try a hundred times or more, and so far, he hasn't managed to land on the board more than twice. Several times he has fallen and landed awkwardly on the kerb. It must hurt. But he gets up and tries again. And each time he seems a little bit closer to getting it right, and I'm filled with a strange pride. I want to cheer at his resilience, and run over and hug him, just like I did when he was a baby learning to walk for the very first time. But then a mean little voice inside me says that you can't make a career in skateboarding and saying 'I can do a 180° ollie' isn't going to get you into university. Surely this is just a waste of time.

I wish I could ride a skateboard. I wish I could look good in baggy jeans and a cool hat. I wish I could spend two hours riding up and down a car park with as much concentration and joy as he does, and not feel guilty about the other things I could be, should be, ought to be, would-like-other-people-to-think-I-was doing. I wish I could ollie. But my skateboarding days are over before they've begun. I'll never match him for balance, for energy, for sheer style. No point in dreaming of something I'll never be. It's just a waste of time.

And as I sit here, hour after hour my impatience melts away. I become conscious that I too am being watched. Watched by a God who lets me fall and try again and fall again and still doesn't give up. Watched by a God who rejoices in the sporadic and incoherent grunts and mumbles I offer by way of communication. Watched by a God who – for no good reason I can think of – chooses to take joy in me, and even when I'm lost in a world of my own, never, never takes her loving eyes off me.

What a joyful, extravagant, glorious, life-giving, waste of time!

Waste your time, but do it joyfully. You are here once.
Wasting time is a sacred activity.

Gilo

9

The Fonger of Blame

*In which I have a nasty accident and
have to work out who to blame*

The Greek philosopher Archimedes said, 'Give me a lever, and
a place to stand, and I will move the earth.' The trouble with
that is that however big a lever you have, it sets you and me
in opposition to a resistant world. The desire to change the
world leaves me with a problem, because it pitches me against
the planet. It's as if I'm over here and the world is over there,
and I want to do something, anything, to change it. The reality
is (as Archimedes knew perfectly well) that I can't act on the
world in that way, because I am not separate from the world.
I am part of it.

One of the least attractive things about Western culture in
the twenty-first century is the almost manic requirement to
find someone to blame for everything that happens. The insurance industry is built on this, and we all know of activities and
movements that have been banned or curtailed because they
couldn't be insured. It seems that there has to be someone to
underwrite everything in case it goes wrong.

We need to accept that sometimes bad stuff happens, and no
one is to blame. One of the characteristics of Everyday Activists is the willingness to go out on a limb, take responsibility,
risk failure and make stuff happen, without being invited to do
so. It's no good getting to the end of your day, your week, your
life and saying, 'Well I could *have moved the world*, but no one
gave me a lever, and I couldn't find a place to stand.'

Excuse me if there are a few spolling mistakes in this chapter. I am typing with a large bandage on my fonger. Let me explain.

I was in a posh London hotel for a business meeting with an important person. Just before we met I went into the Gents to 'wash my honds'. After I had washed them I pulled a paper towel out of the holder and – if you don't like the sight of blood, please look away now – the whole construction fell off the wall. By some random combination of gravity, sharp metal edges and extreme bad luck the towel holder sliced right through the fourth finger of my right hond. 'Ouch,' I whispered, like the self-controlled man I am. In fact, I whispered it so loudly that several hotel staff came running to see what on earth had happened and try to patch me up.

To cut a long finger short, I was rushed to the local A&E, where a nice nurse stitched the end of my digit back on and covered it with a bandage the size of a toffee apple. We men like a nice big bandage. There's no point in cutting the end off your fonger if you're not going to get noticed.

Then an interesting thing happened. Almost without exception, everyone I've told about it (and that includes all the passengers on the West Coast main line and most of the population of Manchester) has asked me the same question: 'Are you going to sue?'

I can't say I haven't thought about it. A posh London hotel must be worth a few quid ... and anyway (as everyone pointed out to me) it will only come off their insurance. But to sue them I'd have to find someone to blame. I guess that's a natural instinct when something goes wrong, but I'm not sure how helpful it is.

A few months back I shut my index finger in my own front door while I was bringing the shopping in. If I'm honest, it was even more painful than my unexpected meeting with the towel holder. But who shall I blame for that? The door manufacturer for making the door too heavy? The child across the street who ran into the road and distracted my attention at the vital moment? Or maybe her parent for not supervising her properly? Maybe I should blame God for sending a freak wind that blew the damn thing shut while my finger was still in the jamb? Or maybe I should stop looking for someone to blame and get on with life with nine fingernails.

Then I thought of Susan, who was disabled almost 50 years ago in a medical accident. She was left bedridden, and for half a century her husband restricted his own life to look after her. It was quite clear who was to blame for her situation, and major financial compensation was an option. But Susan refused to go down that route. No amount of money would have compensated for what had happened to her. But more than that – she didn't feel that going to court and apportioning blame would help her or the doctor who made the terrible mistake. Although she was seldom able to leave her house, her family became a beacon of grace that drew me and hundreds of others nearer to Jesus.

We sometimes ask, 'Why do bad things happen to good people?' The truth is that bad things don't just happen to good people – they happen to everybody. Of course, human beings are responsible for some of the worst stuff. But towel holders just fall off walls because that's the way the world is. Light and darkness are mixed up in ways we do not understand – but through which goodness can sometimes be revealed.

In the meantime, we've created a culture in which someone has to be blamed for everything that goes wrong. And it's not just cuts and bruises. I resent the dentist who put me through such agonies when I was a teenager but still failed to straighten my teeth. I resent the girlfriend who broke my heart. I resent the church leader who made me feel useless. For every regret there is someone to blame. If the value of my house goes down, some politician must be to blame. If my children aren't top of the class, blame a teacher. If my church is less than perfect it must be someone else's fault. The urge to point the heavily bandaged finger is strong. But the little blame industry in my heart has the potential to do me real damage – never mind what it does to the people I'm wanting to blame.

Fingers heal easily, the nurse told me as she dressed it. In fact it's one of the most remarkable things in all creation that wounds of many sorts do heal. And even the wounds that don't heal on earth can sometimes be tronsformed. Hearts can heal too. But not if you constantly pick at the scars.

You have to choose your future regrets.

Christopher Hitchens

10

Meeting Myra

*In which I go to prison and make
an unexpected discovery*

*I don't believe that the world is divided into good and bad
forces locked in cosmic battle like warring chess pieces. Instead
every part of the world is shot through with both good and
evil, like the veins in Stilton cheese. That goes for every human
being too. It would be comforting to think that some people
(like you, perhaps) are irretrievably evil, while others (like me,
obviously) are wholly good. That way we could just work to
get rid of all the bad people, or maybe just lock them up and
throw away the key, and the rest of us could live in peace. The
reality is different of course, and far richer and more interesting
and exciting than that.*

The other day I was standing on our local station waiting for
a train. A bit further down the platform there was a baby in a
buggy, with his mum waiting next to him. Quite by accident
the baby caught my eye and laughed. It made me smile too. So
I pulled a face at him, and he laughed again. At that point the
mum noticed what was going on and quickly turned the buggy
to face away from me.

I don't altogether blame her. I've had my own days of man-
aging buggies in busy places. She probably had enough to cope
with without some stranger pulling faces at her baby. But I
must admit I sighed a little, at this world where an adult can't
look at a baby without raising suspicion.

Before we were married, Jane lived just outside Durham prison. Whenever I went to visit her flat I had to walk past the heavily guarded gates, with their floodlights and security cameras. I don't know about you, but there's something about walking past a prison that always sends a shiver down my spine.

One day a group that I belonged to was invited to go inside the prison and visit some of the inmates. It was a new experience for me – I'd never been in a prison before. We were escorted, of course; through the great wooden doors at the entrance, and then through one clanging gate after another into the prison yard. All around us there were men peering out of high windows to see who was visiting today.

But we weren't visiting the men's part of the prison. We were taken across the big square courtyard and into another building. It was effectively a prison within a prison. Here the security was different. There were no keys, just electronic locks that were opened by a guard watching us via closed circuit television. This was the high security women's prison, where Britain's most dangerous female prisoners were kept. The women – about 20 of them – lived together in just one large L-shaped room with cells around a landing above. It was as grim a place as you could imagine. There was almost no natural light – just a high window, through which I could see the flagpole on the top of Durham Cathedral. Even though it was the middle of the afternoon, most of the women were wearing dressing gowns. I suppose there was no good reason for them to get dressed.

Inside the women's prison I got chatting to a number of inmates. They were keen to talk. I guess we provided a bit of distraction from the boredom of day-to-day prison life. I spoke to one woman for about a quarter of an hour. She was unremarkable in every way. Wearing a quilted dressing gown of the sort that many women wore in the 1980s, she looked not unlike my mum. We had been asked not to speak to the women about what they were in prison for, so we just spoke about this and that – a rather strained kind of small-talk mostly. I remember asking her if she knew what was below the flagpole that we could see through the cell block window. She said she didn't. I told her that it was one of the most beautiful buildings in the world. She shrugged. Then it was time for me to leave.

As I left the prison one of the warders spoke to me. 'Do you know who that was you were talking to?'

'No.' I had been so shy that I hadn't even asked her name, and she hadn't volunteered.

'It was Myra Hindley.'

My stomach turned a somersault. The name Myra Hindley may not mean much to anyone younger than 50, but for my generation, Myra Hindley was an icon of evil. She was jailed for life in 1966 for murdering two children and helping her partner Ian Brady to murder three more. They had tortured the children, recording their screams and photographing them as they did so. The judge at their trial described Myra Hindley as 'a sadistic killer of the utmost depravity'. Growing up I had learnt never to mention her name to my parents, because it produced a visceral reaction in my dad. He had heard on the radio the tape of one of the children being tortured. I'm not aware that my father ever hated anyone, but I think he probably hated Myra Hindley. Like many people of his generation he saw her as a traitor to humanity, and especially to women as mothers and carers. A police mugshot of her, wearing a coat, with blond hair and a staring expression, was seared into my own mind growing up, as a totem of wickedness.

She hadn't looked like that iconic photo as she sat a few inches from me, chain smoking, now with long dark hair and hooded eyes. For a quarter of an hour I had been speaking to the woman who committed some of the most terrible acts imaginable. How could I not have known? Why wasn't it somehow obvious? She hadn't looked a bit like the infamous photograph I'd seen so many times. The shocking thing was that she'd looked – well, normal. Unremarkable. Average.

The accidental experience of meeting Myra has been one of the formative moments of my life. It taught me the hard truth that the worst of humanity looks exactly like the best. On one side of the prison wall lived my fabulous wife-to-be. On the other side lived Myra. The distance between them really wasn't that great.

It would be comforting to believe that the world is divided into them and us; heroes and villains; good people and bad people. That way we can easily reassure ourselves that we are on the right side of the line. I worked for many years in the media, and it was our business to simplify things in this way. All we have to do is round up the bad guys and lock them all up, or declare war on them, or vilify them in the tabloid papers. But of course, the reality is more disturbing. In each of us there is the potential to achieve great things, even if those great things are small and personal and nobody much knows about them except us and God. And each of us has the potential to do enormous damage too, in big public ways or in small private ways: to ourselves, to those we love, to the world around us. So even if we built a thousand prisons, it's simply not possible to lock away all the world's evil. All that's best about being human and all that's worst is all mixed up in each one of us. And that includes me.

Even if I'd never met Myra I guess I might have learnt that lesson from my children. I love Ruth and Ben to bits. I'm not exaggerating if I say that there's nothing in the world I wouldn't do for them. And yet (is it just us men who experience this, or does it happen to women too?) there have been times when I've been so angry with them that I've had to walk out of the room just to stop myself doing some real damage to them. If Jesus really meant it when he said, 'Whoever is angry will be subject to judgement', then I plead guilty. There's a part of me that should be taken straight to the nearest top-security prison. If he was serious when he said, 'Anyone who says, "You fool!" will be sent to hell', then I've earned my ticket there many times.

Myra Hindley died in 2002. Many years have passed since our chance meeting. I'm sad to say I'm beginning to forget what she really looked like. The image of the real Myra is fading, and it's being replaced in my mind by that horrible photograph with the staring eyes that you probably remember too. But I promise you, when I met her she looked no different from you and me. It really *is* only the grace of God's that makes the difference.

We're inclined to look just at the surface of people. We paint them in black and white, or at least a very limited range of colours. Goodies and baddies, friends and enemies; she's smart, he's stupid, vote for him, bomb him. But every person, from the US president to the lump in the bed next to you, is a mass of complex and subtle details, marked by a million experiences that you and I know nothing about. Probably if we could see beneath the surface the depths and the details would astound us. Maybe there are some people we'd be gentler with. Probably we'd stand in awe of every person we met.

Our deepest fear is not that we are inadequate. Our deepest fear is that we are powerful beyond measure. It is our light, not our darkness that most frightens us. We ask ourselves, 'Who am I to be brilliant, gorgeous, talented, fabulous?' Actually, who are you not to be? You are a child of God. Your playing small does not serve the world. There is nothing enlightened about shrinking so that other people won't feel insecure around you. We are all meant to shine, as children do. We were born to make manifest the glory of God that is within us. It's not just in some of us; it's in everyone. And as we let our own light shine, we unconsciously give other people permission to do the same. As we are liberated from our own fear, our presence automatically liberates others.

Marianne Williamson

11

Crossing the Road

In which I have to decide to whether to go with the crowd

I have few memories of primary school, but one or two stand out quite clearly. I remember getting caught up in a playground dispute with a kid called Kevin Burns that ended with a catfight between us. The teacher, in a hurry to get the other children back to their classes, separated us deftly. Without stopping to ask what we were fighting about, or to dispense justice, she immediately declared that we were both equally in the wrong, and insisted that we say sorry to each other. We did, but I left the playground with a burning sense of injustice. Sharing the blame equally between us solved the teacher's problem, but it failed to recognize that I had been wronged by Kevin Burns.

Here is something uncomfortable about Everyday Activism – but something that I can't avoid. You have to pick sides. Activism is not utilitarian. It is not a matter of striking a balance, or finding the via media. *Nor is it about assessing which side would be more comfortable to fall in with. Justice demands that you decide which end of the seesaw you are going to put your weight on.*

Sometimes it is not obvious where justice lies. In those cases, it is tempting to weigh in behind whichever team looks likely to win. Everyday Activists do the opposite. We default to the team that looks weaker, and more likely to be oppressed. If in doubt, we trust the kid with the bloody knees and the scared look in his eyes. It goes without saying that that's not always easy. As a

73

general rule, the harder it feels to join the cause, the more likely it is that you have picked the right one.

When I was in my mid-20s I was a youth worker in County Durham. The miners' strike was drawing to a bitter close, and I was trying to work out how the gospel I had learnt on Saturday nights at my university Christian Union could make any sense to teenagers in an ex-pit village outside Chester-le-Street, whose chances of ever getting a job, let alone going to university, were about the same as my chances of becoming a coal miner. Out of the blue I was invited to a conference in London. It was called the Senior Evangelical Anglican Leaders conference. No one loves a meaningless acronym like Senior Evangelical Anglican Leaders. I honestly didn't know why I was invited, since I was none of those four things. But I was still trying to work out who I was, and I was flattered to be asked, so I went along.

The conference was held at Westminster Chapel in London. It's an austere Victorian building, with a wide frontage that opens directly onto a narrow London street with a slim pavement, just a couple of hundred yards from Buckingham Palace. The whole church was packed with Senior Evangelical Anglican Leaders – about a thousand of them, the great and the good of evangelicalism. Someone once said to me that if you could see now every sausage you are ever going to eat, you would never touch another one. I feel the same about Senior Evangelical Anglican Leaders. They're fine one at a time, but a thousand of them all together turn out to be quite hard to stomach. It turns out that Senior Evangelical Anglican Leaders are about 98 per cent men – at least they were back then. It felt a bit like I expect heaven will feel like – if your idea of heaven is a thousand clean-shaven white men in black shirts and British Home Stores jackets singing Graham Kendrick songs on repeat. I felt like a lion in a den of Daniels. I sat on a pew near the back on the far left. I hadn't chosen it for political or theological reasons, but with hindsight it seems quite appropriate.

The chairman was the Rt Revd Michael Baughen, the Bishop of Chester, and the main attraction was Dr George Carey, the recently appointed Archbishop of Canterbury. I remember the bishop gave his boss a long introduction that seemed more like a grandfather giving unsolicited parenting advice to his son. Now that they had got their man into the top job, the delegates were keen to impress on him how important it was that he didn't let them down. Eventually the Archbishop got up to speak. He'd hardly opened his mouth when there was a crash of splintering wood at the backdoor behind me. There was some sort of scuffle going on in the lobby. There was shouting, and whistles blowing. One or more bodies crunched into the wooden doors of the church. The IRA's mainland bombing campaign was at its height, so most people of my age were used to being evacuated from buildings or even hearing bombs going off, and my heart raced a bit. But I figured that if this was my time to catch the bus to heaven, I stood a chance of stowing away with a thousand Senior Evangelical Anglican Leaders. If you're going to die, die next to the Archbishop of Canterbury.

The next minute, the doors at the back of the church burst open and a dozen men in black jeans and white t-shirts made their way down the aisle. Some were blowing whistles, and the others were chanting rhythmically 'Church of hate, church of fear, stop crucifying queers.' It was the human rights campaigner Peter Tatchell and some colleagues from *Outrage!*, a group that had a public reputation for outing gay bishops. I remember thinking 'Church of hate, church of fear, stop crucifying queers; that doesn't actually rhyme.'

They made their way to the front of the church, but there was only one set of steps up to the platform, and they were blocked by a junior bishop intent on martyrdom, or perhaps hoping for promotion. So instead of going onto the platform,

Peter Tatchell and friends stood in a line across the front of the church, chanting.

The atmosphere was pretty tense. The Archbishop had left the podium looking flustered, and was sitting with the dignitaries on the stage. A loud voice from somewhere near the front started to pray that God would remove the enemy from our midst. They were quite literally trying to pray away the gay. At that point the Bishop of Chester stood up at the lectern. He had the considerable benefit of a microphone, and he said to the assembly, 'Let's sing "Shine Jesus, Shine".' So, whilst a dozen gay protesters in jeans and t-shirts shouted that they were being crucified, a thousand vicars sang *a capella* at the top of their voices that the light of God's love was shining, filling this land with the Father's glory. The protesters couldn't compete. Eventually they made their way back up the aisle and out of the building, from the shadows into the radiance of the sunshine outside. There was no doubt that the Senior Evangelical Anglican Leaders had won this round. I caught one young protestor's eye as he walked out, and I recognized the look of brokenness mixed with defiance. I'd seen it in the eyes of many young people in my ex-pit village in the north east.

I can't remember what the Archbishop's talk was about, or how it was received. It didn't seem to matter any more. *Blaze Spirit, blaze. Set our hearts on fire.*

When it was finished we all filed out through the splintered back doors. Peter Tatchell and his few companions were standing immediately opposite the building, on the other side of the road. They weren't chanting any more. The police had penned them behind metal barriers. It meant that as we walked out of the building, each Senior Leader momentarily found themselves looking directly into the eyes of the protestors no more than 20 feet in front of them.

As we gaze on your kingly brightness, so our faces display your likeness. One thousand evangelical leaders, and every last one had to make a choice. As you left the building you could turn right, towards Buckingham Palace; or you could turn left towards the bars and cafes of Westminster. Left or right; sheep or goats. Or you could walk straight ahead to where a dozen queer men were holding makeshift posters saying that you were crucifying them. *By the blood I may enter your brightness; search me, try me, consume all my darkness.* Almost every one of us turned either to the left or to the right, to disappear into the local cafes or head for the tube. Just three people didn't turn left or right, but walked straight across the road to meet the protestors. One was John Gladwin, then the Provost of Sheffield Cathedral. The second was Michael Vasey, a gloriously gay evangelical leader whose blue homburg hat and red felt blazer stood out in the sea of black jackets and dog collars, in the midst of the darkness, shining. And then there was me, understanding for the first time the connection between my jolly university faith and the downtrodden young people of the pit village in Chester-le-Street. I knew that if I didn't cross this road now, nothing about my Christian faith would ever make sense again.

You can safely assume you've created God in your own image when it turns out that God hates all the same people you do.

Anne Lamott

12

Eight Voters Can't Be Wrong

In which I decide to stand for parliament

Winston Churchill famously said that 'Democracy is the worst form of Government – except for all those other forms that have been tried.' He said it in the House of Commons in 1947, though he wisely prefaced it with the words 'It has been said that …' It's a great get-out to attribute an idea to some other anonymous person. That way, if it turns out to be a bad idea you can always add '… but what do they know?' at the end. I can't blame anyone else for my decision to stand for parliament. It was my idea, and mine alone. And although (spoiler alert) I didn't win my seat, I don't regret it. Everyday Activism can't only be about gestures. We have to be prepared to roll our sleeves up and get stuck in.

Lots of people have told me that they couldn't stand for parliament because they can't agree 100 per cent with any of the political parties. That strikes me as rather too easy. If we can only work with people with whom we wholly agree, we're not going to get much done. I once cheekily asked the veteran Labour MP Frank Field whether he had ever compromised his beliefs and values in the course of his political work. He looked at me wearily. 'I've never achieved anything without compromising my beliefs and values,' he said.

I guess sometimes, in the real world, we have to make a choice between being right and doing good.

I vividly remember the day I told my future mother-in-law that I intended to marry her daughter. She made me promise just one thing – that I would never become an MP. I've no idea why she said it. Such a ridiculous, extravagant, arrogant idea couldn't have been further from my mind. I was busy working as a youth worker, and also trying to make a living as a freelance TV producer and radio presenter. Standing for parliament isn't a smart career move. It's not a hobby. It takes over your life. I can't for the life of me remember what possessed me to do it.

The idea to stand came out of the blue. True, I had been marginally involved in local politics. I had delivered Labour party leaflets on the street where I live and once even stood as a 'paper candidate' in the local council election. But I hadn't knocked on a single door and I certainly didn't have a rosette. I'd simply allowed my name to appear on the ballot paper in a no-hope ward so that the party could show willing. And that was the sum of it. A general election is very different.

As tradition dictates, I looked for a seat that was completely unwinnable (or as the party modestly described it, 'challenging'). Cheshire's Hazel Grove constituency was next door to the constituency I lived in, so it seemed ideal. It had been firmly Liberal Democratic since 1997, with the Conservatives in second place. So I could truthfully tell my constituents that I was fighting to win, whilst confidently keeping my promise to my mother-in-law.

I found the name of the constituency secretary and rang him. He wasn't sure how the system worked, but asked me to send him a CV. I did, but heard nothing for weeks. I imagined I was being secretly checked by party officials looking for skeletons in my cupboard. In fact, they had lost my form. Still, the next thing I knew I was invited to a selection meeting with party members at the local Labour Club. This was campaign launch, my Super Tuesday.

Stockport Labour Club is a dreary building off the A6. It consists of a small bar, and a large meeting room where they hold small meetings. The floor is sticky with spilt beer, the furniture looks like *The Rovers Return* circa 1950, and – I kid you not – there are posters on the wall advertising rallies to be addressed by Kier Hardie. 'Welcome to the Labour Club,' said a man behind the bar. 'This is where old party members come to die.'

I stood next to a kindly-looking lady at the bar and offered to buy her a drink. I was just being polite. 'You can't do that,' she said earnestly. 'That's bribing the electorate.' This seemed the best excuse I'd ever heard for not buying your round, and I decided there and then to make full use of it. I let her buy me half a pint. It seems it's not OK to bribe a voter, but fine to do it to a potential MP.

The task of selecting the candidate fell to the eight party members who had turned up, plus an energetic young official from the regional office. 'It's my first time doing this,' he said to me, eagerly. 'Mine too,' I said. I hoped I wouldn't let him down.

Also at the meeting was Brian, the other candidate. It turned out that he lived in the constituency and was a member of the local party, which meant he could have a vote, while I, from the constituency next door, couldn't. This seemed a little unfair. A quick calculation indicated that, assuming he voted for himself, he was 12.5 per cent up on me before I'd even opened my mouth. I had everything to play for.

Brian was summoned to make his speech first. He was obviously a seasoned campaigner, having stood for and won a local council seat. I, on the other hand, had never made a political speech in my life. I waited nervously outside, listening to the scattered applause from the group as Brian addressed them.

I was eventually called in and gave my speech, which I had written in my head on the way to the club. At the end there was some polite clapping. I was then bombarded with questions. I soon worked out that whatever I said, three of them would agree with me, and the other four wouldn't. The only sensible option was to say what I truly believed about each issue. The problem was knowing what that was. My political education came from 20 years of reading *The Guardian* and listening to the *Today* programme on Radio 4. It wasn't enough. What did I think about the monarchy? God bless 'em – I think. Trident? Do we still have that? The Middle East? Yes-but-no-but. Grammar schools? Erm, my son goes to one. At the critical moment, I discovered that I didn't actually have a view on most things that couldn't be changed by a smart argument from the other side. I'm still not sure whether this is an obstacle to political office, or a qualification. When my time was up, I left the room and rushed to the toilet, convinced that my political career was over before it had begun.

Three minutes later the voting was finished. The man from the party was clutching a shoe box with a slit in the lid, held together with sticky tape. He asked the two candidates to step forward. Then he asked for three volunteers to act as tellers. With only eight votes to count, that seemed a bit excessive. But rules are rules. So four of the electorate stayed in their seats while six of us gathered round to watch the tape being ripped off the box.

From where I stood I couldn't see the face of the ballots, but I could see that they were being sorted into piles – well, one pile actually, neatly stacked on the left of the table. Then they were returned to the middle and carefully counted again, this time eight little slips in a pile on the right of the table. Then it was all done.

The party man turned to the group and said that I had been duly elected as candidate for the Hazel Grove constituency. There was polite applause. He invited me to make my acceptance speech. I spoke nobly about the privilege of representing them, how no seat was unwinnable and how the campaign would be all about teamwork. They looked at me with what I now realize was a mixture of weariness and pity. It may have been my first time as a candidate, but they had all been here many times before, and the wonder was that they had bothered to come here again.

Afterwards the man from the party took me aside to fill in a form accepting the nomination. I had to declare, among other things, that I didn't know anything that would embarrass the party. It occurred to me that selecting a candidate with eight voters was pretty embarrassing. I'm not sure I was supposed to see it, but the form said the vote had been unanimous – I'd got all eight votes. In other words, even the other candidate had voted for me. Thanks, Brian. If I can only repeat that pattern across the constituency, I thought, the election will be a shoo-in. If I can pull off the same trick nationally, dictatorship is not out of the question.

With the form filled in, the Labour man left. I turned to thank my supporters and encourage them that together we would fight a strong campaign. But they had gone home. I walked out, and made my way to the bus stop. It was late, and the buses had stopped running, except for the 192 to Hazel Grove. I took it, right to the heart of 'my' constituency, and walked home from there.

On 5 May 2005, the day of the general election, I campaigned outside the local primary school, toured polling stations all morning, then went to the Labour Club to encourage party workers. There weren't any. So I went home and decorated the downstairs bathroom instead.

Meanwhile, 39,117 people turned out to vote in Hazel Grove. Remarkably 6,834 of them voted for me. That's more people than had voted Labour in Hazel Grove for three decades. Thank you, thank you, all of you. Only another 12,500 and we will be almost there. I have no idea who voted for me of course; indeed, on election day I got a charming letter from a constituency officer, one of the eight who had selected me, saying that – nothing personal, but he wouldn't be voting for me this time. Still, one day I will tell my grandchildren that I was a parliamentary candidate at the May 2005 election. On second thoughts, I may keep it to myself.

Some victories are hollow, but some defeats are glorious.

Paul Vallely

13

It's OK to Show Some Emulsion

In which I attempt to make the world a better place, using a ladder and a bucket of emulsion

On my first day at High School, at ten years old, I was dropped at the school gate in my blazer and cap. I was blond-haired, blue-eyed and whatever the opposite of worldly-wise is. I looked like something out of Just William, *and couldn't have been more eager to please. The very first thing that happened was that I was presented with a little book. It contained all the school rules – about 30 pages of them as I recall. It had been designed to fit in the breast pocket of my blazer. The implication was clear. Keep this next to your heart; keep the rules and you will win the approval you so desperately want. I went home after that first day feeling like it wouldn't matter a jot if I never passed an exam, just as long as I didn't run in the corridors or walk up the down staircase.*

I still don't make a habit of breaking rules. My school experience succeeded in making me instinctively compliant. But you can't be an Everyday Activist if you are not prepared to walk on the wrong side of the line sometimes. Everyday Activism is transgressive. It is all about doing what the rest of the world says should not be done. Sometimes that's being generous when the world says you should hold back. Sometimes it is coming close to a person the rest of the world tells you to avoid. And sometimes it involves creeping about at dead of night with a ladder and a bucket of emulsion.

The 2005 Conservative Party election campaign was the dirtiest of my lifetime. The Tories had been out of power for a decade, and they were desperate. They ran with the umbrella slogan, 'Are you thinking what we're thinking?' which, come to think of it, we might as well fix as the compulsory message for all parties at all elections. That way we could have it printed up on posters and just bring them out every five years.

I was particularly aware of how dirty the campaign was because I had accidentally found myself standing for parliament as the Labour candidate for Hazel Grove. I say accidentally, because I had been selected by the unanimous vote of the eight members of the local party. That in itself was quite remarkable, as one of the eight was standing against me. When it came to it, it seems he didn't even have the confidence to vote for himself. But that's another story.

Jane and I had recently moved to South Manchester, to a colourful multicultural community where Bangladeshi, Pakistani, English and Irish cultures mixed together in a glorious soup. Michael Howard's Conservatives ran a highly divisive campaign. As a result, we woke up to find that the billboard high up on the railway bridge beside our house had been plastered with a huge poster – a plain white background with black lettering three feet high proclaimed: 'It's not racist to impose limits on immigration.' I was outraged. It may or may not be racist to impose limits on immigration, but to put that poster high on a bridge in a multicultural community was clearly a dog-whistle intended to cast migrants as a problem to which a Conservative government was the solution. I imagined how that would feel to people from non-English cultures as they saw the message every day. Every time I walked under the bridge it made my blood boil.

Fed up with a boiling husband, the ever-practical Jane asked me what I planned to do about it. And so a plan was hatched. We realized that there was only one word on the poster that we had a problem with – the word 'not'. And it occurred to us that with a pot of white paint and a roller we could correct it for them. And that's how, at 1am, the parliamentary candidate for Hazel Grove and his wife were seen walking along a street in South Manchester with a ladder, a paint roller on the end of a broomstick and a large bucket of emulsion left over from doing the kitchen ceiling. We had all of the ingredients for a Laurel and Hardy tribute act.

For a middle-class boy from Croydon, it felt incredibly furtive to be carrying a ladder at dead of night. I was dreading a police car driving past and stopping us to ask what we were doing. I could see the headlines on the next day's papers – election candidate caught … well, doing what exactly? Breaking and entering? Snooping into upstairs windows? No, Officer, we were just taking the ladder for some fresh air.

When we got to the bridge we realized the job was going to be more difficult than we had anticipated. First – the poster was considerably higher than the ladder. And second – the billboard was surrounded by an 8-foot-high metal fence with spikes on the top. Even to get close to the poster we would need to scale the fence and drop down to the other side, somehow bringing the ladder and the paint over with us. And third – the poster was floodlit. We were going to have to do all of this in full West End lighting.

We propped the ladder against the fence and I climbed up, shielding my eyes from the glaring lights. Carefully negotiating the spikes, I balanced on top of the fence. I reckoned I could drop down onto the grass below without getting hurt. Jane could pass the roller through the fence, but the paint would have to follow me over the top. Jumping off an 8-foot fence is one thing. Jumping off an 8-foot fence with a bucket of emulsion is going the full Chuckle Brothers. Then we realized that if Jane kept the paint bucket on *her* side she would be able to load up the roller, then pass it through the fence. This might just work.

While I balanced on top of the fence, Jane pushed the

ladder up the outside, then pivoted it over the spikes and let it down the other side. Then I slid down the inside of the fence. Success. I was now inside the metal cage, with the roller and the ladder. My wife was on the outside with a bucket of white paint. Momentarily it occurred to me that if Jane wanted to get revenge for the last 25 years of marriage to me, this was probably the best opportunity she would ever get.

I opened the ladder to its full length and propped it up against the hoarding. It was a ridiculously steep angle. I'm not good with heights. Jane loaded the paint roller and passed it through the fence. I climbed the ladder. Even at the very top, with my arm extended over my head and holding on to the very end of the roller, the paint would only just reach the word 'not'. To get the paint to cover the word I had to bounce on the ladder. I didn't dare look up, and anyway the light was blinding me. So I just took a rough aim, looked at the ground and by a sort of bobbing motion, aimed the roller at the word 'not'. I could feel the watery paint running down the pole of the roller, over my hand and down my sleeve. Splashes of paint dripped onto the back of my head. I had a fresh appreciation of the way Banksy suffers for his art.

We reloaded the roller two or three times for good coverage. Each time I had to descend the ladder and climb up again. Then, more from exhaustion than completion, we decided to call it a night. I passed the roller back through the fence, climbed over and pulled the ladder back. Then we walked home again and fell into bed, feeling we had made our stand against white nationalism.

When I got up in the morning I walked out to the scene of the crime. The cheap paint had run down the poster, as if some enormous bird had dumped a watery load on it. The word 'not' was still clearly visible, if a little greyer. 'It's not racist to impose limits on immigration.' It's not sensible to climb a ladder with a pot of paint in the middle of the night either. But some things just have to be done.

A seed can have no concept of what it is like to be a plant.
Yet even in its ignorance, it will still become one.

Veronica Zundel

14

Parts of Me Are Dying

In which I learn to love my cancer

Nobody, I hope, still believes that illness is sent as a sign that God is angry, or that a person gets sick because they have sinned. But I have always wanted to be one of the solid ones – the sort of person who adds value by caring for others and contributing to the community – a net giver instead of a net taker. It was having cancer that taught me the joys of being loved and cared for by some of the most gentle and generous people I have ever known. Strange that in all the years I have known them I'd never given them the chance to care for me like this.

More than anything I was nervous about admitting to myself that I was ill. I don't like appearing vulnerable. Nearly everything in my upbringing has told me that I should be strong, that I should achieve, that I should lead. When people ask, 'How are you?' I instinctively said 'Fine.' When they said, 'Are you keeping busy?' I answered 'Yes.' But sometimes I am not fine. And busyness is a rubbish way to gauge usefulness. As a tiny act of rebellion against a culture that demands strength, I am learning to receive my weakness, and all the limitations that go with it, as a gift. To do that is revolutionary.

One of the great skills that's worth learning early in life is how to pee when you want to and not when you don't. To be honest I've never been that great at this for as long as I can remember. I went to an all-boys' school where you were basically divided into sets in Year 1 according to who could pee highest up the wall. I soon got the message that I would never amount to much, but I learnt to cope. When I look back on it I had an amazing range of coping strategies. For more than 30 years I would never, but never, go into a building without checking out where the nearest loo was. I would always order the smallest possible drink in a pub. I would insist on the aisle seat in the cinema. If there was anybody sitting between me and the exit I could have a serious prostate-related panic attack. I would catch a bus rather than a tube because if I had to, I thought I could open the emergency doors and jump out. This is an issue that I suspect lots of men have, but we just don't like to talk about it. I remember once it got so bad that I rang the Incontinence Helpline. You won't believe this, but the Incontinence Helpline had this answerphone message saying 'Your call is in a queue. Please hold on.'

I have total sympathy for Gérard Depardieu, the French actor who had prostate cancer. He was caught short once on a plane about to take off. The flight attendant wouldn't let him undo his seatbelt and go to the loo. Believe me, I've been there. You're sitting there making desperate plans – and the only receptacle within reach is the free bottle of water they gave you. And you're thinking, 'If that was empty, I could pee in it. But the only way I can get it empty is to drink it.' Nightmare.

In my early 40s it had got to a stage where it was just plain awkward – especially if, like me, you make your living as a live broadcaster. It was time to see a doctor.

I ended up in a small windowless corridor in a hospital in Manchester on 23 December. I'd been waiting there such a long time that a nurse came up and suggested I go to the tea bar for a cup of tea. I kid you not, they were serving tea in mugs with signs of the zodiac on them. Guess which one I got? Here's a clue ... it begins with C. Turns out it wasn't just a drink, but a diagnosis.

Anyway, eventually I saw a doctor. There are three ways they test to see if you have prostate cancer. The first is a blood test – which is a reasonable guide but not definitive. The second test is you have to bend over, and the doctor puts his finger up your bum. He does that because apparently you can actually feel your own prostate. Imagine that. I thought I knew my own body reasonably well, but I was nearly 50 before I found that out. And the third test is a biopsy, where they use an endoscope to scope your end, and nick bits out of you to examine under a microscope.

Once I'd had all three I went to see the doctor. By this time, you'll understand, I had quite a close relationship with him, although I'm not sure I'd ever met him face-to-face. Anyway, he looked up from an orange cardboard file with my name on the front of it and said, 'You have cancer.' I think he said some other things too. In fact, he must have done, because I was in there for over an hour. But to be honest that was the only bit I remembered – the only bit that really seemed to matter.

So, now I knew. I had cancer. The cancer I had was quite small, quite early and quite treatable. But it was cancer and I had it. Prostate cancer. Not a very glamorous cancer, but by no means the most destructive either.

I had thought of prostate cancer as an old man's disease. Most people who get it are about 20 years older than I was. But I figured, 'Why wait? Have it while you're young enough to appreciate it.' My own prognosis was much better than some people's. In fact, the doctor said, 'There's an excellent chance you'll die of something else first.' Thanks, I thought.

You might ask what a prostate is. Every doctor explains it in the same way. They say, 'it's like a mini-doughnut.' Great. So now I knew I had a mini-doughnut up my bottom. Not even a proper full-size doughnut. A mini-doughnut. Like you get from the bakery counter at Sainsbury's. With the chocolate dip. Now, not only did I have prostate cancer – but I was put off doughnuts for life.

Several things happen when you discover you have a cancer. First of all, there are some things that happen *to* you.

When I left the surgery I felt like I had a tattoo on my forehead saying, 'I have cancer.' I felt like everybody would instantly know about it. I felt like the human race was divided into two groups: those who have cancer and those who don't. On my way home from the clinic I went to the supermarket to do the weekly shop. The disjunction between cancer and Tesco seemed immense. I found myself pushing my trolley down the aisle looking for the check-out queue for people with cancer. I felt sure we must have separate arrangements.

I caught myself continually thinking about the fact that I had cancer. At first it was almost constant. Then for about three months, I thought about cancer at least once every hour. After a couple of years, I got it down to about once every three hours.

I don't want you to get the impression that my life was dominated by cancer. It really wasn't. I wasn't even very interested in cancer. And in many ways, nothing had changed at all. It was like an unwelcome visitor with really bad personal hygiene who butted in on every conversation and didn't know when it was time to leave. But my autobiography, if I ever write it, will be divided into life before cancer and life after.

When you have cancer there's a choice of treatments, a bit like the menu in some macabre restaurant. 'Would sir like the radical surgery? I can offer a 90 per cent chance of chronic incontinence with that. Or will you start with the radioactive implants? That comes with a side order of erectile dysfunction. Of course, you could have nothing at all. Some of our customers have lasted as long as ten years that way. Though of course you wouldn't want to come back for secondaries.'

Then there are some things that my cancer seems to do to other people.

Some friends didn't know quite how to react. It made them feel awkward. Well-meaning friends started to tell me their cancer stories. I honestly lost count of the number of times someone said to me, 'There was a time when the doctor thought *I* might have cancer.' And I had to say, 'Well, I guess there's a subtle but very important difference between you and me then.' One lovely person gave me a cheery book on how to avoid getting cancer by eating nothing but broccoli. Hmm. A bit late, perhaps?

A lot of people seemed to treat it like a new hobby I'd taken up that they couldn't quite approve of. It's as if I'd said I'd decided to experiment with witchcraft; or I was teaching myself to fart the 1812 Overture. Some people didn't even like to use the word. They said things like, 'How are you coping with your ... [nod] ... you know ... problems?' So I'd say, 'It's fine thanks. As long as I keep up the payments ...' One friend I hadn't seen for ages asked me gently how my chemotherapy was going. I had to remind her that I wasn't having chemotherapy. This is what my hair normally looks like.

Telling colleagues at work was difficult. In a competitive world I was nervous that I would turn out to be the wounded zebra that is picked off by the hungry hyenas. In fact what happened was that a number of colleagues sidled up to talk to me for the first time about the stresses and strains they were carrying. It hadn't dawned on me before that by accepting the narrative that health and strength are virtues, we put pressure on everyone around us to live up to those unrealistic standards, or worse still, to disguise their own weakness. I guess that's why, rather notoriously, we tend to avoid talking about cancer at all if we can. Cancer is the Voldemort of diseases, the Scottish Play of sickness. You'll be aware of the circumlocutions we use to talk about cancer. The C word; the Big C – a phrase that was quite probably coined by none other than the archetypal film tough-guy John Wayne.

Some people were incredibly generous. Some lovely friends of ours decided we needed a break, so they sent our family for a fortnight in Florida. We went to Disneyland ... the whole works. Did you know, if you go to Disneyland and you have cancer you can get a badge that lets you go straight to the front of all the queues ... *if* you're a kid. So I was there with this grave illness, and my daughter was there, and it happened to be her birthday. She got a big badge. I got nothing! All day long it was 'Happy Birthday, Ruth' and 'Have a nice day, Ruth' and I thought, 'Excuse me. She may be the lead singer but it's me that got us the gig.'

Here are some of the things I discovered. Number one: God is good. Number two: my lovely church mattered even more than I thought it did. Number three: the NHS is wonderful, but when they say quarter past two they really mean ten past four. Number four: I had cancer. Did I mention that?

I was really struck by the kind of rhetoric that surrounds cancer. Cancer has its own linguistics, and it's all very aggressive. We talk about fighting cancer or battling with cancer. I heard a radio interview with the footballer John Hartson, where the interviewer said he had 'kicked cancer'. We speak about cancer like an invading force that needs to be repelled. When the broadcaster Chris Evans went for a cancer check, he came away saying, 'This type of enemy is one hundred per cent beatable – provided you don't give it a chance to fire the first shot.' Hang on a minute. What's this about beating and shooting? That's just not my kind of language. Recently I read the obituary of a colleague, and it said that he had 'lost his heroic battle with cancer'. I felt there was a clear expectation on me to fight this cancer – to be a hero – even though, inevitably, I'm one day going to lose the fight. The thing is, I'm not really the fighting type. I'm virtually pacifist. The language of battling doesn't have any appeal for me. I don't want to be called a cancer victim, because I don't feel I am a victim. Nor am I a hero.

I was confirmed as a fourteen-year-old in the Anglican Church. The man who confirmed me happened to be the Anglican Bishop to the Armed Forces. I remember asking him, as a cocky teenager, how as a bishop he could justify supporting armed conflict. He said to me that the world was cancerous, and that there were some parts of it (by which he meant some people) that could only be dealt with by cutting them out. Even then I was a bit shocked. Looking back, I wonder whether the language of cancer and the language of warfare are actually reinforcing each other?

I read an article in the *Daily Telegraph* that said that the 15 Tory MPs planning to vote against their party's whip were 'a cancer within their party'. And I thought, 'Why take it out on cancer again?' Why not, 'The measles within their party'? Measles is much more infectious than cancer, but like bad journalism, it can usually be treated. Why not, 'The halitosis within their party'? Bad breath is something we can all do something about. But no – it's cancer again.

The language of war dominates cancer discourse. Whether we want to fight or not, people with cancer are conscripted into a battle against the self, our bodies made into war zones with cancer as the enemy, medical professionals as infallible heroes, and treatments of search-and-destroy by any means possible. We don't objectify other diseases like this. We don't treat a stroke as an alien invasion, or go to war on our own heart disease.

The rhetoric extends to the doctors too. Oncologists are painted as heroic figures, the SAS of the medical world, only they use other weapons – sometimes hand-to-hand fighting with scalpels, sometimes a much more space-age battle using lasers and ray guns.

In 1971 US President Richard Nixon signed into law a National Cancer Act. It was known as The War on Cancer. Nixon set the stakes high. 'The time has come in America,' he said, 'when the same kind of concentrated effort that split the atom and took man to the moon should be turned toward conquering this dread disease.' They even converted a biological warfare facility in Maryland into a cancer research centre. But in spite of $100 billion of tax-payer funded research in the US alone, the cancer mortality rate hasn't shifted all that much.

Don't get me wrong. I didn't want to have cancer. It's a bad thing in so many ways. I wish every biological warfare centre in the world was converted into a cancer research centre. But I warn you that when I die, if anyone says that I have 'lost my battle against cancer', I will personally come back and haunt them.

Why do we do this with cancer? I think what happens is that when we are dealing with something we don't understand and can't see, the temptation is to create a mythology around it. So we give it a persona: cancer – the enemy; the alien invader. We treat it as a beast or a parasite. We give it a godlike or demonic status. We fear it. Then – if you have had cancer you'll know about this – we ask ourselves whether we have done something to deserve it. Had I sinned: eaten too much; not exercised enough; smoked the wrong stuff? Was it my fault? Then we curse it, or we pray to it for mercy. In all of this we externalize cancer. We make it separate from us.

But the cancer I had was *my* cancer. It was part of me. These were my cells – albeit they were doing me damage. The pain or discomfort that I had was not an alien attack. It was my body signalling that something was wrong – trying to come to terms with itself – dealing with its own situation.

If I say that I have cancer I'm already turning it into an outside abstract force. Most doctors don't even use the word 'cancer' to each other – because it's so abstract and generalized as to be virtually meaningless. I didn't have 'cancer' – I had 'a' cancer. More particularly I had 'my' cancer. My very own, that was part of me, that I was giving hospitality to, albeit reluctantly. These were *my* cells. OK, they had gone wrong and they were trying to kill the rest of me. But they were mine, and I loved them. Turning them into some sort of objective enemy and declaring war on them would be just self-destructive.

I'm not saying that anger is inappropriate here. You may well be angry that you have a cancer, or that others who you love have a cancer. That seems to me to be a perfectly justifiable anger. But I'm afraid there isn't an actual 'thing' for you or me to be angry at.

So how should I treat my cancerous cells? They were part of me – but they were confused. Just like all my other cells they were struggling for survival. They were a bit dim, because they hadn't worked out the longer-term consequences of what they were doing … that if they managed to survive and colonize the whole of me I would die, and then they would too. The poor little cells needed loving back into line – with strict discipline if necessary. St Francis of Assisi, who had long-term illness himself, is said to have spoken about his 'Sister Illness'. He embraced his illness like a family member.

At first, the treatment I had for my cancer is what the medics called Active Surveillance – another quasi-military term. Basically it meant that we did nothing but watch the cancer as it grew. Given that the side-effects of more invasive treatment would include chronic incontinence and impotence it seemed like a reasonable choice for a forty-nine-year-old. Still, one lovely friend rang me up to say, 'I hear you are refusing treatment for cancer.' That was astonishing on several counts. First, it suggested that there had been some conversation somewhere where he and others were discussing my cancer treatment. Then there was the suggestion that I am some sort of conscientious objector in the war against cancer; so refusing treatment might make me either a) heroic or b) naive, according to your theological preference. But I was neither heroic nor naive. I was just a man with a cancer, like so many other people. Sister Illness had come to stay.

Maybe all this is sounding a bit weak. The reality was that parts of me were dying. I asked a doctor friend how many cancer cells we were talking about. I was hoping for a couple of dozen at most. He reckoned several hundred thousand at least. Still, it was fair to say that 99.5 per cent of me was perfectly well. It's just that the other 0.5 per cent was trying to kill me.

But hang on – I'm only going to die the same number of times as you or anyone else. The reality is that parts of all of us are dying. That's built into the design. Is it possible that we should think of cancer as just one of the natural ways that the body ends itself? Maybe it's an evolved feature of the human race (and of pretty much all the other multi-cellular forms of life).

I'm not expecting to die soon. But I am expecting to die 20 years sooner than I thought I would, and that concentrates the mind. Having my cancer made me ask myself what I really believe will happen to me after I die. Given that I'm going to spend at most another decade or two being alive and then an awful long time being dead, it seems like a good thing to consider.

All my life I've had some sort of picture of life after death. Probably as a child I thought of heaven in a fairly crude way – a place where I would live for ever as a reward for giving my life to Jesus. And alongside that I had a picture of hell: a place where my brother would go for ever as a punishment for being two years older and disproportionately smarter than me. Strange to say, according to that view, dying was all good news. As the old spiritual goes, 'If you get to heaven before I do; tell those angels to pull me through!' It couldn't happen soon enough. As a teenager I remember praying that Jesus would come back soon and very soon – although not before I had had sex. Or during it.

As I grew up, my notion of what would happen to me after I died got a bit vaguer and a lot gentler. I guess that I believed that God would sort things out in the end. I did some serious Bible study at university and decided that I no longer believed that Jesus had talked about hell as an active, enduring punishment. Still, according to that view, dying was good news of a sort, because it meant I could be with Jesus – and it overcame the risk of a chronic misjudgement whereby my brother might have ended up in heaven while I went to hell, and had to eat cauliflower for ever.

As I went further, my notion of any sort of after-life got vaguer still. I think by the time I was in my forties I didn't really believe that there was any future after I'd died at all. I had to work out what to do with all the stuff Jesus said about heaven and hell, but I studied theology in the 1980s, so I was highly trained in how to use spiritual language to talk about the stuff I didn't actually believe. I saw that as a positive step that went alongside the politicization of my faith – the belief that what God cares about most is the here and now, issues of justice and practical caring. According to that view what happened when I died really didn't matter at all, since I wasn't going to be there, but what happened while I was alive mattered very much. Indeed, what happened while I was alive was all that could possibly matter.

There was a reason for that. At the time I lived on a downtown South Manchester housing estate called Adswood where the human need was raw, and injustice was built into people's lives. It seemed to me that dealing with that injustice was what faith was about. The idea of saying to people who were impacted by bad housing and inadequate healthcare that there was a heaven they could aspire to seemed really wrong, and especially so if it meant saying that I was going to be there but they might not.

Now I realize that my Adswood friends were trying to tell me something. In Adswood pretty much everybody believed in heaven, and in angels, and often in hell too. At the very least there was a sense that God would see that justice was done in heaven, when it patently wasn't being done on earth – at least not in Adswood. Lots of people marked the death of a family member with a small ad in the paper saying something like: 'We miss you but we know you're looking down on us.' I think I'd lost any sense of that at all, and I don't think I'm alone. When they heard I had cancer, why did not one of my middle-class friends talk to me about the hope of life after death? Not one. In fact, why did so few of them talk to me at all?

Is it possible that the reason I and so many of my friends don't talk about heaven – or any form of life after death – is that we've lost our belief in it? If so, is that a good thing? A bit of quasi-spiritual superstition jettisoned along with believing in the power of God to find us a parking space? Or had I lost something totally central and vital, without which the rest of my faith really didn't make sense?

I suspect that all the language about fighting cancer, a war on cancer and so on comes from a particular myth of human progress that we have massively bought into. It's what you might call the doctrine of evolutionary optimism. It's the idea that took root in the Enlightenment that the human species can and will continue to succeed and improve. To believe that, you need to believe that the only things that are really bad are the things that stand in the way of human health and growth and happiness. And you have to believe that all of those can be conquered in the end by human craft and intelligence. Why is cancer a problem to society? Why did Nixon declare a 'war on cancer'? Because it offends the doctrine of evolutionary optimism. Cancer has been so stubbornly unbeatable that it's taken on a mythical status. As a result, everyone who gets cancer is unwillingly conscripted into the army of individuals who must play our part in the fight against it – not necessarily just for our own sake, but as part of the wider battle to prove that human beings won't be beaten.

Sometimes we do manage to win the odd battle. Sometimes a person becomes cancer-free. Sometimes a whole group of cancers is pretty much subdued (although not destroyed). But cancer is a bit like Al Qaeda – it's more an idea than a defined reality, so although we can win some battles with it, and eliminate it from some places, we can never declare it beaten. All of that places a huge unnecessary burden on those of us who have cancer. Not one of us ever really wins our so-called 'battle with cancer'. And as far as evolutionary optimism goes, we're all letting the side down.

Several people have encouraged me to fight my cancer, but I'm not the fighting kind. I just happen to be a man who had cancer. Make no mistake, I wanted to get rid of it ... the sooner I saw my prostate in a jam jar, the better. In the meantime, my prostate cancer was no more or less than a pain in the bum. I didn't want to fight cancer. I wanted to live really well with cancer ... and then hopefully to live really well without cancer.

At church the Sunday after my cancer was diagnosed we read Psalm 103: 'Bless the Lord, O my soul, and all that is within me, bless God's holy name.' I was brought up short. What, *all* that is within me? Even that handful of pesky cancer cells? Are they supposed to bless God's holy name too? How exactly does that work? Then it occurred to me that I have choices to make. I choose to lift my hands in worship sometimes. I choose to open my mouth and sing. I even choose to dance from time to time (at which point my kids usually choose to look away and disown me). And I choose that everything within me shall bless his holy name ... including my cancer cells. I'll let you know when I've worked out what that means.

Here's my faltering attempt to be going on with. Suppose cancer is part of the way the world is meant to be. Trees drop their leaves in Autumn. Some animals are predatory on other animals. The sun goes down at the end of the day. There's a sadness about all of those things, but not a wrongness. They aren't in themselves evil. We need to avoid the sense that all material things are evil because they decay and die, but all spiritual things are good because they last for ever. Does that mean that scientists should put down their scalpels and stop looking for a cure for cancer? Not at all. Life would be better without cancer, without pain, without sickness. But not without death. Death is not the enemy. The enemy is despair.

I think I started out my Christian life with a layered view of the universe. Earth in the middle of the sandwich – all the material things I was experiencing here and now – with heaven above and hell below – both of them intangible and spiritual. Somewhere along the way I lost all the spiritual stuff altogether, and practically speaking I only believed in earth, which mostly sucked, but could sometimes be made better. Now when I read the Bible, I find a different picture altogether. Again and again I find that it speaks about heaven written *through* earth like the letters through a stick of rock. Heaven in earth *now*. And the battles, which are real, are not between the material and the spiritual. They are about who or what we will worship and bow down to. Cancer, you may come and be part of me, and I will host you. But I will not worship you; I will not be defined by you; I will not dignify you with a fight.

It seems to me that the Bible doesn't say that I have a soul that will survive when my physical body comes to an end. Instead what it says is that God is creating a new heaven and a new earth out of the very physical cells of our existence. I have the delightful prospect that one day my little handful of cancer cells will be resurrected, transformed, reshaped into something really beautiful – a diamond, perhaps. I'd better look after them. And this experience of living with cancer will itself be transformed into something beautiful – a joke maybe, or a few minutes of hope, or a collection of words in a book.

It seems to me that through much of my Christian experience I've hung on to the very important idea of transformation, but I've let go of the absolutely central idea of resurrection – if I ever had it at all. Every cell of my body will die – there's no doubt about that. It's self-evidently true. But it's not the end of the story.

Recently I sat with my friend Andy who was dying of cancer. Then two weeks later I went to his funeral. As they lowered his body into the grave I thought, 'Is God seriously saying that this body will rise again?' And the answer is yes – not in a Hammer Horror way – but not just in a disembodied spiritual way either. Somehow – the Bible seems to be saying – the flesh and blood that was Andy will be taken and remade in a form that is infinitely better, fuller, deeper, richer – recognizably Andy but much more so. If there's a mystery to be swallowed, then that's it. Because of that my cancer needs to remain very real –

not disembodied or spiritualized but very physical. That way it reminds me of my transience. It signposts me towards the future. It points me from the present to the tomorrow that God has in store. It's a reminder that I am not yet what I can be and will be. It is God's thumb-print on the plasticine of my existence.

I happened to have cancer, but we all have our own individual instances of God's thumb-print in our plasticine. Parts of me are dying, and parts of you are too. All I'm saying is that we shouldn't necessarily isolate those things or demonize them or objectify them, but carry them as marks of the promise of what God will do with us together and apart.

And what about when I die – whether that's next year or in 20 years' time? Well, I don't know what will happen any more than you do. But if you buy the central truth of the resurrection of the body you no longer need to fear death, or run from death, or even fight to stave it off to the last possible moment. To talk about what happens after we die we have to resort to pictures. There's no other honest way. Normally, being an arty type, I'm happy with pictures, but in this singular instance of the very physical death of my cells, I really want a very physical understanding of what's going to happen, and I haven't got it.

One picture has been helpful to me, though it's not perfect. Imagine you were walking down the street and you came across a pile of broken glass. Clearly a window has been smashed. I live in Manchester – we know about these things. The good thing to do, I guess, is what thousands of so-called 'Wombles' did after the riots in Manchester a few years back, which is to get a broom and clear up the glass and put it in the bin. But God is doing what no human being could. God takes the fragments of glass and reassembles them into a perfect pane – more perfect and clearer than it ever was before. We are broken glass. We are being remade. The fact that I am broken is irrelevant compared with what I will be, with you too.

So do I believe in life after death? The hell I do. I believe in life *in* death, *out of* death, *before* death, *after* death; life through death and life embracing death. Life throwing its arms around death and loving it to bits.

Religion to me has always been the wound, not the bandage. I don't see the point of not acknowledging the pain and the misery and the grief of the world. And if you say, 'Ah, but God understands', or through that you come to a greater appreciation, I then think, 'That's not God, that's not my God.' I see God in us or with us, if I see God at all, as shreds and particles and rumours, some knowledge that we have, some feeling why we sing and dance and act, why we paint, why we love, why we make art.

Dennis Potter

15

The Time of Your Life

In which I miss the moment ... not once, but twice

Everyday Activists don't believe that life's a lottery. And we don't believe (like some religions) that everything that happens, happens because God wants it to. But we do believe that there are moments of opportunity in life – times when a door opens and you can choose to go through it. The doorbell rings and someone turns up in need of help. Or it could be a chance to forgive an old hurt and rebuild a broken relationship, or a moment when you can reach out for help or healing. But if there are moments of opportunity, there's also the possibility of missing the moment.

For a broadcaster like myself, timing is everything. The programme I present on BBC Radio 4 lasts exactly 14 minutes and 54 seconds. A second less and radios across the country will go silent. People everywhere will think their batteries have run down. A second more and my voice will crash into the 'pips'. Tide and the Greenwich time-signal wait for no man.

Timing isn't always my strong point. A few months ago I had to make an early morning trip from my home in Manchester to Watford, in the south of England. I got up on a chilly Manchester morning and put on my best cold-weather gear ... warm vest, scarf and overcoat. (Aren't you proud of me, Mum? All those years of training paid off!) But as the train went further and further south, so the temperature went up and up until I was sweltering. If I didn't take my vest off, I thought I'd pass out.

Now, the toilets on those inter-city trains are pretty small. There's not a lot of room to manoeuvre, and I had quite a lot of manoeuvring to do. I managed to get my coat and jacket off, undid my trousers and unbuttoned my shirt. Then I got my vest off. And just at that moment the voice over the tannoy said, 'We are now approaching Watford Junction station.' What was I to do? Either I could dive out of the loo and onto the platform half dressed, or I could keep my decorum and miss my stop, and the meeting I had travelled all that way for. I'm not going to tell you what happened, but I'd like to take this opportunity to apologize to the people of Watford for any offence I may have caused.

It is sometimes said that Eskimos have a hundred words for 'snow'. This is, of course, nonsense on stilts (though if you live close to the North Pole, walking on stilts is not advisable). It's hardly surprising that there are a lot of words for snow, just as there are about a hundred words for rain in Manchester. However, it is certain that the Greek language has at least two different words for time, and they imply quite different things. One is *kronos* – from which we get words likes chronological, chronometer and chronic. It means the time in which we normally operate, time measured by clocks and watches. We parcel out our days in kronos time – so many hours till home time, so many months till our next holiday, so many years till I retire. That kind of time passes painfully slowly until you are about 40, then starts to speed up alarmingly. The other Greek word for time is *kairos*. It means a moment of opportunity – the chosen time, the absolutely right time to act.

Denis lived in the flat opposite ours. I saw him going out most afternoons, and I often heard him when he came back in the early hours, long after the pubs had closed. Denis was an alcoholic. He didn't have any friends really, beyond a few drinking partners in the marketplace where he used to go, but I'd often chat with him in the street when he was sober, and sometimes if he saw me getting the car out he'd nip over and I'd give him a lift to the shops. We talked about all sorts of things, but always about his drinking. He knew it was well out of control and likely to kill him. 'Andrew,' he'd say, 'I'm going to book into a drying-out clinic. I'm going to get off the drink once and for all.'

One day Denis came over to the car and asked for a lift into town. 'Andrew,' he said as we drove along, 'I'm going to go to the clinic. I need to get on top of this drinking once and for all.' I pulled over and stopped the car on the side of the A6. 'OK,' I said. 'Let's go now. I'll drive you there straightaway.' There was a look of panic in his eyes. 'Thanks for the offer,' he said. 'Tomorrow. I'll go tomorrow.'

And that was the last time I saw Denis. He collapsed in town that evening and was taken to hospital where he died. His liver had finally failed.

When a great moment knocks on the door of your life, it is often no louder than the beating of your heart, and it is very easy to miss it.

Boris Pasternak

16

Sssssh!

In which I learn to live with constant noise

I have no doubt that if God turned up in person at most churches, the first thing he would say would be 'Turn the noise down!' Most churches would help people to worship God better if they included a few minutes where everyone stopped talking and singing and gave God a chance to get a word in edgeways. 'Be quiet, and know that I am God,' God said to the psalmist. Well, that's all very well, God, but some of us don't have that luxury. If you can find five minutes in a day to shut yourself away and listen to God, or the world, or yourself, please do it. If you can find five days to get away to a convent or walk by yourself in the hills, go for it. As an Everyday Activist I'm all in favour of quiet retreats, wordless prayers and listening for God's still small voice in the silence. But some of us, me included, have to listen for God in the constant noise of our everyday lives.

Even now the children have left home, our house is pretty noisy. I expect yours is too. But these days it's a different sort of noise. The central heating boiler pops on in the morning and makes a low, continuous hum as it warms the rooms. It's always there, providing a layer of sound on which every other sense sits. I live close to a main road, and on a rainy day there is a constant swoosh of tyres displacing water, adding another layer of sound. I'm a radio lover – and it's a rare moment when you can't hear the mutter of indistinct speech from some corner of the house – a third layer of ambient sound blending with the others.

Still, I can remember times that were too warm for central heating, dry enough to silence the traffic, when the children were out at school and I was alone in the house with no radio on. Then there was nothing but nothing; an empty silence in which the mind can rest. Lovely!

I can remember those times, but I can no longer visit them. Last year I was diagnosed with a tumour affecting the balance centre of my left ear. It gives me few symptoms at the moment, except that it presses on the nerves that control my hearing. As a result, I have a constant noise in my head, akin to the boiler plus the traffic plus the distant radio. It's not loud, but it's always there. Bach's piano sonatas are now accompanied by a low drone like a distant hoover. It's as if every word I write, I write onto paper that already has a covering of random marks. Even my silent prayers are accompanied by a humming chorus. 'Sssssh!' used to be the sound we made when we wanted the kids to be quiet. Now, ironically, it's the noise that my own head makes, even when they are not there.

It's strange to think that the signals that create this noise don't relate to anything in the real world outside my head. I'm not actually hearing anything except the interference on the line between my ear and my brain. Most noise has some sort of purpose, but mine is a noise that has no value. It isn't useful. It doesn't offer information or remind me of danger or reassure me that someone is present. I can't share it with you. It is the noise of my own soul.

There are only two ways this noise will stop. I could ask a specialist doctor to treat my tumour with surgery. The likelihood is that if and when I do this, the sounds will end, but so will my hearing. I have the choice of constant background noise or perpetual silence. For today I choose noise. The other way it will end is with my death. One day my whole body will fall silent as I begin to explore new layers of sense that none of us can yet imagine. For today I choose life.

I no longer have the option to choose silence – to stand in a field of virgin snow listening to nothing, or lie very still and hold my breath like I did when I was a child, and experiment with the absence of sound. So instead I choose to live in a world of noise. I notice the sound of the passing cars and their drivers, the raindrops falling on the window ledge, the reassuring radio and the hum of my computer. And I notice moment by moment the sounds of my own flawed internal circuitry, reminding me that I am alive again today – reminding me to choose life.

My Lord God, I have no idea where I am going. I do not see the road ahead of me. I cannot know for certain where it will end. Nor do I really know myself, and the fact that I think I'm following your will does not mean that I am actually doing so.

But I believe that the desire to please you does in fact please you. And I hope I have that desire in all that I am doing. I hope that I will never do anything apart from that desire. And I know that if I do this you will lead me by the right road, though I may know nothing about it.

Therefore will I trust you always, though I may seem to be lost and in the shadow of death. I will not fear, for you are with me, and you will never leave me to face my perils alone.

Thomas Merton

17

A Moving Tale

In which I bet the house, and just about get away with it

Many of us are strongly motivated by security. In the West, that isn't usually a question of food and water; they are not normally in short supply. Instead we want to make sure that we have safe housing and enough money to see us into old age. We put locks on our doors and invest in pensions and savings to ensure we will be comfortable. The prospect of being dependent on family members or others is held up as a matter of fear and shame.

It doesn't have to be that way. What if, instead of running from dependency, we saw it as a gift? After all, we begin life totally reliant on other people. Why shouldn't we keep it that way, celebrating our own weakness and the generosity of others? Everyday Activists are risk-taking rebels. They are reckless with their assets and under-invest in their own security. They over-trust other people, and take the gamble of sharing their lives with the marginalized, the unreliable and the love-hungry. They live lightly, swapping security for joy.

A friend of mine was leaving her house with her three-year-old son to go to Toddler Group. They came out of the house into the little porch and the sneck on the front door locked behind them. Then she reached for the outer door in front of them and realized that that was locked too ... and her keys were inside the house ... and they were trapped ... mum and toddler imprisoned in their own tiny front porch. What a nightmare! And with the little boy. I mean there's only so many times you can sing 'the wheels on the bus go round and round'. After three hours she had completely run out of ways of entertaining the toddler. Then the little boy had a brilliant idea. He looked around the little six foot square porch and he said, 'I know mum – let's play hide-and-seek!'

They were in there for five hours before they were rescued by a passer-by who called a locksmith to let them out. Ever since then, I've checked very carefully that I've got my keys in my pocket before I leave the house. It's a powerful thing to have a set of keys. I've got my car keys in my pocket, and I've got my house keys, and I've also got the keys to the building where I work. As long as I've got the keys I've got authority to go in and out of those places whenever I choose.

I'd been married about six months when Dave came into my life. To be honest I hardly knew anything about him. I just knew that he was a big guy – I mean really big: a biker, with a mass of curly black hair and tattoos running down his muscly arms and peeping out from the neck of his shirt. Plus, I knew that he was homeless. Well, strictly speaking, he wasn't homeless; he was living in a nearby hostel known as The Spike. It was a series of corrugated iron huts, each containing 12 iron beds, 12 chairs and 12 men whose lives had gone catastrophically off course. The Spike was cold, miserable and dangerous.

I was going off to stay with my mum and dad over Christmas, and it just didn't seem right to leave my house empty while Dave was going to be sleeping in The Spike, so I gave him a set of keys to my house, left a phone number and told him I'd be back in the New Year.

Half-way down the M1 I began to wonder if I'd been a bit naive, but by that stage there wasn't much I could do about it. Over Christmas I got more and more worried. I mean, what if he'd been holding wild parties; what if he'd trashed the house;

what if I came back to an empty shell? By the time New Year came and I was driving back up the motorway towards my house my heart was in my mouth, wondering what I'd find.

What I found was this big bear of a man, grinning on the doorstep. Dave had hoovered, washed the kitchen floor and had a chicken dinner waiting for me in the oven. As we sat and ate together, Dave told me his story, and my mouth dropped further and further open. It seems he'd spent his adult life as a pretty-much full-time burglar. The reason he was homeless was because he'd just finished his latest spell in prison for house-breaking.

As he finished telling his story he was beginning to fill up. 'You see,' he said, 'I've never had the front door keys to a house before. No one's ever trusted me like that, so I made up my mind I was going to look after your house like it was my own. I owed it to you 'cos you trusted me.'

There was nothing heroic about me trusting Dave with the house. It came out of ignorance and naivety. But trust begets trust, just as suspicion begets suspicion: that's true of human relationships between friends, between neighbours, and even – perhaps especially – between nations. For that cycle of trust to begin, one party has to take a risk – to trust someone, knowing that it might just end in disaster.

'By the way,' he said as we finished our late Christmas dinner, 'I couldn't afford to get you a present … so I thought I'd give you the benefit of my professional services instead.'

'You don't mean you've nicked something for me Dave?'

'No,' he said. 'I'm trying to put all that behind me. But I've given your house a thorough check over from a burglar's viewpoint. A sort of personal security consultation. And I'd say you've got nothing to worry about.' And with that advice from a top pro, I slept easy in my house from then on.

When our children started at high school, we moved house again. We wanted a place where they could have their own rooms, so we ended up with four bedrooms. The house was bigger than we strictly needed, but we were hoping to adopt, so it made sense to leave some 'growing room'.

That was then. Fifteen years later our youngest moved out, and Jane and I were left rattling around a house that was too big for us, which we could barely afford. My job was coming to an end too, and we didn't know what the future would hold. We decided it would make sense to downsize. We wanted to stay local, so we put our house on the market and started looking for something smaller nearby.

If you've ever tried to sell your house, you know it has a potent effect. We cleaned constantly – even cleaning places we hadn't touched for years. We painted walls and did everything we could to freshen the old place up and make it look attractive. Crucially, we started chucking things out. I made a painful decision to reduce my book collection by a third. We went through cupboards and sent old clothes to the charity shop. And as the *For Sale* board went up at the end of the drive, we started saying our goodbyes to lovely neighbours and friends.

After a bit of to-ing and fro-ing we accepted an offer on our house, and did a deal on a smaller house a mile or two away. A moving date was set and we booked a removal van. All our books went into crates, which were stacked in the hallway by the front door; all our pictures came down off the walls, leaving tell-tale shadow marks behind them; we started to pack the clothes we wouldn't be using for a few months.

Then, just 48 hours before the removal van was due to roll up the drive, an email from our buyers pinged into my inbox. They were really sorry, but they were pulling out of the move. The deal was off. I had to read the email about six times before it really sank in. We were going nowhere.

The first and worst thing I had to do that day was to visit the house we were hoping to move into, and tell the poor shocked family that our move was cancelled, and so theirs was too. Then I had to unpick all our arrangements with the solicitors and the removal firm. Then I had to go round and tell all the neighbours that they were stuck with us a bit longer. A lot longer, as it turned out. The mortgage broker made it clear that now I had no fixed income they weren't interested in offering us a loan on a new house, even a smaller one. We were stuck. While Jane and I sat on the packing cases in the hall, wondering what on earth was going on, a man came to take down the *For Sale* sign from the front gate.

Later that morning the phone rang. It was an old friend from work. She and her husband had found themselves with nowhere to stay and wondered if we had a room they could borrow for a while. As it happens, we did! They arrived next day to find us re-hanging pictures and putting books back on shelves.

Within the next few days we had a call from a local organization working with asylum-seekers. Marion had arrived in the UK from Burundi. She was a children's worker, but was fleeing for her life having been threatened by her government. She had nowhere to go. Could she stay with us? She did.

Marion was followed by Lai from China, Rosanna from Zimbabwe, Sophia from Somalia, Yasamin from Iran and Meru from Tibet. Some have stayed for a few weeks; others for many months. They have become our friends. They have been joined by students coming to the UK to learn English: Maria from Peru, Hisako from Japan, MiHo from Korea and a score of others. Visit our house for dinner (and I'm not just saying that; please *do* visit our house for dinner) and you will find a veritable United Nations gathered around the table, swapping stories and making friendships across the divides of language and culture.

Of course, there are downsides to having a full, international house. Sometimes there's a queue for the shower. Sometimes the cutlery gets put in the wrong drawer and you can't find the potato peeler. But there are so many upsides. Fantastic smells of international cuisine waft through the house at all hours. We hear stories and see pictures from places we never knew existed. And we now have a network of friends in every continent.

Gifts come in many forms. Money, yes, but also time, trust, door keys and even spare rooms.

As I get older I seem to believe less and less, and yet to believe what I do believe more and more.

Bishop David Jenkins

18

Bird

In which a small bird learns a big lesson

When I was a child there was an old pumping station at the end of my road. Day and night two huge beam engines driven by five steam boilers heaved a million gallons of water every day from deep beneath the North Downs to supply the people of Croydon. At weekends the station was open to visitors, and I can remember watching in amazement as the vast beams rose and fell with an almighty crashing noise. The sheer power of it was quite literally awesome. It's rare to feel so close to a source of such power, and as an eight-year-old child I just wanted to say 'Wow!'

The steam-powered pumping station stopped working long ago, but sometimes I wish I could recapture a bit of that childish wonder. Things have changed. The mobile phone I carry in my pocket, for instance, has more computing power than the Apollo rocket that landed on the moon, and I take for granted the immense power I have at my finger-tips. Even in an age of plenty, Everyday Activists need to retain our sense of awe and dependence.

The other day a tiny bird flew in through our bedroom window. I got the shock of my life, and so did the bird. I was just standing there, when suddenly it arrived, perched on the window frame for a moment, then dropped like a stone and started flapping around on the bedroom floor. I don't know which of us was more surprised. The poor little thing was panicking.

It obviously hadn't got a clue what to do, and to be honest, neither did I.

So I did what I usually do in moments of crisis: I called my wife. She picked the bird up, softly cupping it in her hands, and gently lifted it up to the open window. It was flapping like mad. Once her hands were outside the window she opened them flat. The bird stopped flapping for a moment and just waited. It was almost as if it needed a moment to get its thoughts together. Then it launched off and flew away.

Later on, I wondered what the bird made of the experience. What did it tell its parents when it got back to the nest? All right, I might be getting a bit 'Walt Disney' here. David Attenborough would probably tell me that birds aren't as philosophical as all that. But I wondered whether it had any sense of having been rescued, held, delivered by something bigger than itself. There's something curious about that sense of being held in hands that are much bigger than your own – hands that could crush you but instead choose to support you. Some people call that faith. I don't know whether birds have the capacity to feel grateful. Probably not, but I know that humans do, and I am. I hope that little bird goes through life with a nagging sense that there is something bigger, much bigger, than itself; and that once upon a time, that something that could easily have harmed it actually helped it instead.

We are not yet what we shall be, but we are growing
toward it;
the process is not yet finished but it is going on;
this is not the end, but it is the road.
All does not yet gleam in glory, but all is being purified.

Martin Luther

19

One Day

*A song celebrating the future,
when we will live at peace*

When I turned 40, I made some life-changing discoveries. One
of them was that for 40 years I had been wearing shoes that
were too big for my feet. Why? Because every time I walked
into a shoe shop to buy a new pair of shoes, I heard my
mother's voice ringing in my ears, and she was always saying
the same thing: 'You must leave plenty of growing room.' It's
what she always said to me when we went out to buy school
shoes together when I was a child, and it stuck with me like a
mantra. So much so that, even though I'd been buying my own
shoes for a quarter of a century, even though my feet stopped
growing when Harold Wilson was Prime Minister, I'd still been
buying shoes with plenty of growing room for all these years.

The annoying thing about it is that my mum was right, of
course. She was trying to teach me something important: to
buy my shoes and live my life with an eye to the future. But by
keeping that idea fixed in my mind I'd done the exact opposite.
Every time I bought a pair of shoes I'd been stuck in the past,
and as a result I'd ended up spending a quarter of a century
wearing shoes that didn't fit.

I've never liked detective stories – never had the time for
them. But a friend of mine persuaded me that this was a gap
in my education and I really ought to try. Scanning his bookshelves, he pulled out an Agatha Christie novel and gave it to
me, with the strict instruction that I was to read it straight

through from the beginning, and on no account was I to jump to the end and find out whodunnit.

So I did. I read faithfully through, staying in the present, with an eye to the future. I followed all the twists and turns of the plot, trying to pick up the clues and keeping the last chapter firmly closed. It was a yawn ... but I kept my word. Then I got to the last scene. All the characters were gathered in the Drawing Room with the detective. He was just about to reveal the name of the murderer. I turned the page and – the last couple of pages were missing! Some joker had torn them out. So that's me done with murder mysteries. After all that effort I never did find out whodunnit.

Some religions teach that history goes round in circles. Some people believe that we can be reincarnated, possibly many times. Christians believe that history unfolds like the pages of a novel – that it is not like the London Eye, but the London Marathon. The end of the story is already written, and it's fortunate for us that we can have a sneaky look at the last chapter. We can know how the story ends, and it is good news. History is purposeful. It had a starting point, and it is moving inexorably towards an end that is fixed. Since it's not endless, it is not aimless. Christians believe that history is moving towards a time when God will renew the earth, cancel out all that we've done to spoil it, and bring his people together to live in peace. Our lives fit into that progress, whether we know it or not, and nothing we can do will stop it.

Every summer along with thousands of others, I go to the Greenbelt Festival. Like all the best festivals, Greenbelt is held outdoors. If it rains, everybody gets wet. If the sun shines, everybody gets warm. Being out in the elements is a great leveller.

By nature, a festival is a temporary community. It is provisional, and experimental, which makes it a good place to try things out. For most of us, 95 per cent of the year is spent getting by – making the machinery of life work for us and those around us. At a festival you can ask questions that you wouldn't dare to ask the rest of the year. You can say, 'Where is all of this heading?' You can ask, 'What would it be like if we did things differently?' That's why people wear stuff at festivals that they wouldn't be seen dead in the rest of the year. If it's not too pretentious, I would say that a festival is a place where we prefigure the future by building a temporary model of heaven in a field in Northamptonshire.

One of the centre points for every Greenbelt Festival is the Sunday morning communion service. It's not like any church service you have ever been to. There's no priest, no altar and no hymn book. It is an inclusive, creative gathering of up to 10,000 people who meet in a field to see what they can find in common, and celebrate it, using the ancient Christian symbols of shared bread and wine. In 2016 the whole of the event was hosted from start to finish by children. They prayed, sang, told jokes and led people ten times their own age in diverse and play-ful worship. It was a beautiful symbol of the upside-downness of the Christian vision of society. At the heart of the celebration was this song, 'One Day'. The song points ahead to the time when God will bring the whole of creation to completion. It is based on a fantastic picture in the Bible that speaks of a time when 'Wolves will live in peace with lambs, and leopards will lie down to rest with goats. Calves, lions, and young bulls will eat together, and a little child will lead them.' (Isaiah 11.6, International Children's Bible).

Feel free to sing it alone or together, and of course, to make up your own words.

'One Day'

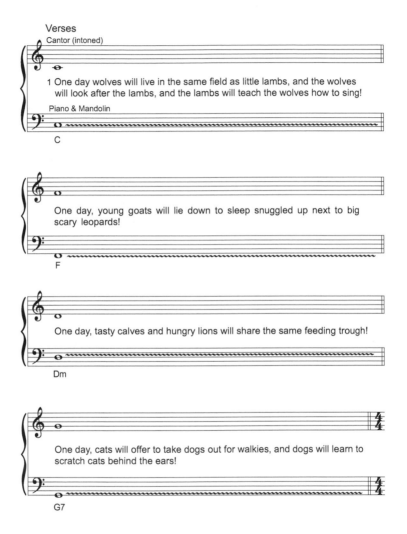

Verses

Cantor (intoned)

1 One day wolves will live in the same field as little lambs, and the wolves will look after the lambs, and the lambs will teach the wolves how to sing!

Piano & Mandolin

C

One day, young goats will lie down to sleep snuggled up next to big scary leopards!

F

One day, tasty calves and hungry lions will share the same feeding trough!

Dm

One day, cats will offer to take dogs out for walkies, and dogs will learn to scratch cats behind the ears!

G7

ONE DAY

Chorus

One day, one day, per-haps it will be [Sun-day],

Wood block
Bass drum   Bass guitar

C   F   C   G

one day we will live in peace and a   lit - tle child will lead   us.

C   F   C   G   C

Kazoo: doo, doo, ...

C   F   C   G

F   C   G   C

One day wolves will live in the same field as little lambs, and
the wolves will look after the lambs and the lambs will teach
the wolves how to sing
One day young goats will lie down to sleep snuggled up next
to big scary leopards
One day tasty calves and hungry young lions will share the
same feeding trough
One day cats will offer to take dogs out for walkies, and dogs
will learn to scratch cats behind the ears.

One day, one day, perhaps it will be **Sunday**
One day we will live in peace and a little child will lead us.

One day the Jedi and the Sith will join forces and use the
Power of the Force for the good of the galaxy
One day Draco Malfoy will invite Harry Potter round to his
house for Lego and a sleepover
One day, PCs will say to Macs, 'Have I ever told you how ele-
gant you look?' and Macs will say to PCs, 'That's very kind,
but I owe everything to you in the first place.'
One day men and women will be paid the same amount for
doing the same job. Simple as that. Nothing else to say about
that one really. End of.

One day, one day, perhaps it will be **Saturday**
One day we will live in peace and a little child will lead us.

One day Tom will make friends with Jerry, and Sylvester will
stop chasing Tweety Pie
One day He-Man will shake hands with Skeletor, and Batman
and the Joker will join forces to clean up Gotham City
One day the Montagues will invite the Capulets over for tea
and say how nice it is going to be to be one big happy family
One day the Beales and the Mitchells will sit down for Christmas Dinner together in Albert Square and nobody will throw
anything or call anyone else a muppet.

*One day, one day, perhaps it will be **Friday***
One day we will live in peace and a little child will lead us.

One day the fans of Manchester United and Manchester City,
Rangers and Celtic, Liverpool and Everton will sit side by side
on the same terrace and cheer when each other's teams score
One day the biggest bully in the school will walk home hand
in hand with the smallest kid and the smallest kid will help
the bully do their homework
One day brothers and sisters will share their toys, and not
argue over who has to go to bed first or what they want to
watch on TV
One day kids will laugh at their dads' jokes – without
even trying.

*One day, one day, perhaps it will be **Thursday***
One day we will live in peace and a little child will lead us.

One day women will be able to walk home at night, and
if they hear footsteps behind them it will only make them
feel safer
One day men and women, gay and straight, will share
everything from changing rooms to churches
One day no one will be interested in what kind of school you
went to, or whether you went to university, or what your
father did for a living
One day prison doors will be flung open, and prisoners and
the people they have hurt will throw their arms around each
other.

*One day, one day, perhaps it will be **Wednesday***
One day we will live in peace and a little child will lead us.

One day politicians from every party will sit around in a circle and work together to bring about justice

One day the people of America will embrace the people of
Mexico, the people of Britain will swap recipe tips with the
people of Europe and the children of Syria will work together
to rebuild their country
One day Protestants and Catholics will worship side by side
in a language they don't even understand, and no one in the
Church will feel the need to talk about gender and sexuality
any more
One day there will be a black James Bond – or even Jamelia
Bond for that matter.

*One day, one day, perhaps it will be **Tuesday***
One day we will live in peace and a little child will lead us.

One day Democrats and Republicans will listen to each other
to choose a leader they can all respect and trust
One day all the passport booths at ports and airports will be
replaced by welcome desks where someone with a smiley face
tells you how glad they are that you're here
One day the fact that you are black or white, Hutu or Tutsi,
Sunni or Shia will be nothing more than an interesting topic
of conversation
One day the wall between Israel and Palestine will be torn
down, and all the children of Abraham will live side by side
in peace.

*One day, one day, perhaps it will be **Monday***
One day we will live in peace and a little child will lead us.

One day, one day, perhaps it will be
Sunday ... Saturday ... Friday ... Thursday ... Wednesday ...
Tuesday ... Monday ...
One day we will live in peace and a little child will lead us.

Those who were seen dancing were thought to be insane by those who could not hear the music.

Friedrich Nietzsche

20

Faith, Hope and Mischief

Laughter is infectious. However bad the joke, if someone is really creased up, it's almost impossible not to laugh with them. It's a big mistake to try to do religion, politics, activism or sex without laughter. Take Julian of Norwich, the fourteenth-century mystic who was, as far as we know, the first woman to write a book in English. Julian was an anchoress, meaning that she spent her life alone, voluntarily walled-up in a cell. When she was extremely sick and expecting to die, she had a vision of the love of God. It hardly sounds like comedy gold, but in her vision she says:

> I laughed mightily, and that made all those who were with me laugh also, and their laughing made me happy. I wanted all of my fellow-Christians to see what I had seen, so they could all laugh with me. But I did not see Christ laugh, for I saw that our laughter is for our own comfort, rejoicing in God that the devil is overcome.

What seems to have set Julian of Norwich off here is a radical vision that in the end good has and will overcome evil. It's a theme repeated in her writing, and it goes well beyond mere hope. This isn't the hollow cackle of an empty universe but the joyous belly-laugh of someone who's just worked out how the world's joke ends.

I want to laugh, and I want to change the world. There are a number of reasons for this. The main reason is that I have lived long enough and travelled widely enough to know that the world is grotty. More than that, the world is seriously messed up, trashed, unfair and full of sadness and disappointment. Every one of us has to find a way of dealing with that fact. There are essentially only two options. One way is to insulate yourself from as much of the horror as you can. That's not easy to do in a highly-connected age, where news reaches us from every corner of the world faster than Usain Bolt can run. We tend to be aware of tragedies within minutes, even if they have happened the other side of the world. What is more, all the tragedies are mixed up. A devastating hurricane can sweep across a vast swathe of Asia, killing tens of thousands and leaving communities devastated. The ten o'clock news may cover it for three or four minutes, provided there are pictures to illustrate the item. Then the next item on the bulletin may be the anguish of a child's death from neglect or disease much closer to home. The stories are on a wholly different scale. Every death is equally tragic, but edited together they make a brown mess of heart-breaking calamity that seeps into my soul and makes the world seem cruel. And even as I watch the news bulletin, I know there is not a single thing I can do to make life better, either for the grieving parents of the child or for the thousands affected by the hurricane, so for the sake of my soul, to enable me to get through the day at all, I insulate myself against it. I don't do that by avoiding the news altogether. That seems to me to be a form of betrayal, but I have to do something to cope. I simply don't have enough emotional battery life to feel all the things that would be appropriate to feel in response to all these disasters, especially as I haven't yet processed the disasters I heard about yesterday and the day before. So instead of closing my eyes and turning away, I learn to dial down my emotional response. Now, after 50 years of learning about the devastating awfulness of so much that happens around the world, I am able to hear about agonizing grief, unbearable disasters and insufferable injustice, and still go on to watch a comedy programme, or make spaghetti, or pet the dog as if nothing much has happened. I'm not saying this with any sense of pride. In fact, I'm saying it with shame. But in practice, this is how I make the world's tragedy tolerable – by allowing it into my soul in only a homeopathic dilution. What else am I to do?

Still, I want to change the world. Is that so much to ask? The second reason why I want to change the world is that I want it to be better for my children (and for their children, and their children and so on). I'm not selfish enough to want it better only for my children, but I don't like to imagine that with all the knowledge we have of human psychology and all the technology we have available to us, the world they inhabit in, say, 50 years' time will be just as grotty as the one we have today. I want to think that the world is on a path of improvement. Unfortunately, the realist in me knows that this isn't the way things go. I distinctly remember my physics teacher telling me at school that by the time I was 30 all human beings would be issued with jet packs so that we could transport ourselves from place to place. Well, Mr Harle, not only were you wrong about the jet packs, but have you seen the traffic on the M60? Also, when I was 20, I genuinely thought that within my lifetime the appalling patriarchal bias that my generation inherited would be done and dusted, and there would be equality between the sexes. How wrong was I? Fifty years on, it feels as if that dial hasn't shifted much at all. So I'm not optimistic about the short-term future. My desire to make the world better for my children and grandchildren is simply based on the fact that I feel like my generation hasn't been that impressive in tackling the challenges we were set, and the very least I want to do is make sure the next generation has a better shot.

The third reason why I want to change the world is entirely selfish. I want to be significant. I don't want to feel like I have passed through the world without making a mark. Something inside me says that this whole thing will be worthwhile if I can make some definite improvement. I'm not looking for much: a cure for cancer, perhaps, or an end to world hunger. I'm not picky. But I do want to tip the world's see-saw in the direction of good, even if it's just by a couple of degrees. To be frank, that part of me mostly wants to make the world better so that I can feel better about myself. I'm being really honest with you here. I want to do something great to validate myself.

The more I burden myself with the idea that I should change the world, the more I find myself pitched against the world's built-in powers. For a start, changing the world starts to look like a race against time. When I was 20 it all looked perfectly feasible. I had ages to make a difference. Now I'm almost 60 and confidently past half-time, I feel like the clock is against me. I don't want to wholly abandon the idea of changing the world, but nor do I want to succumb to a feeling of hopelessness as the window of opportunity slowly closes.

It's not only time that is against me either. If my settled purpose is to change the world, I'm really going to need to accumulate quite a lot of raw power. I'm well aware that to change the world you either need to have a vast brain so that people will bow to your superior intellect, or you need to have political influence that can get things done on a national or preferably a global level, or you need to have enough money to buy the change you want to see. Stephen Hawking had a huge brain; Greta Thunberg has massive political influence; Bill Gates has almost limitless supplies of cash. I haven't got any of those, and I haven't really got enough time left to get them. But I still want to change the world.

Recently, a friend of mine, who is a prominent campaigner, told me that if I want to make a difference I need to 'build my personal brand'. What he meant was that I need to leverage whatever power or personality I have, through social media, through writing, through my friendships and contacts, to make sure that I am projecting myself into the world in a way that I choose, and a way that people will take notice of. I see lots of people who are prominent in public life who do just that.

They take great care about the ways they present themselves, and by doing so they build a platform from which they hope to do great things. But what if the best way to change the world is not through collecting power, but through rejecting it. This runs counter to almost everything I was taught at school, and also to all of the hidden assumptions that I have picked up along the way. What if the best way for an Everyday Activist to exercise power is sometimes to get out of the way?

A few weeks ago a female friend told me something that blew my socks off. She simply described to me her experience of walking down a busy street. She told me that all the time she walks through a crowd she is pausing, dodging, and moving out of the way to avoid bumping into people. She said that this is an experience shared by lots of other women. Men simply expect to be able to walk in a straight line. My friend said that she had tried, as an experiment, to walk down a street the way that men do – looking confident and not moving aside for anyone. She found that she was bumping into people all the time, because they expected a woman to get out of their way.

At first I was dubious. I'm 59 now, and I've been walking on busy streets since I was about 18 months old. I don't think I'm a pavement bully, and I couldn't believe that I had missed something so obvious. So for a few weeks I tried to observe how men and women negotiate busy places, and I discovered that my friend is right. On average, men seem to walk in straight lines while women dodge and weave. I've since noticed the same thing in children's playgrounds and in supermarkets too.

One of my most profound values is that women and men are created as equals. That's a challenge in a world where men still have all sorts of advantages just because we are men. In our society, men disproportionately occupy senior jobs, which means that we have disproportionately higher pay than women. And that's just the start of it. Imbalance runs through society from the office block to the pavement and from the Houses of Parliament to the playground.

Putting radical equality into practice in an unequal world will be uncomfortable. In my experience it's hard enough to deal with inequalities that stare us in the face. It's much harder to tackle the privileges we aren't even aware of, like having priority on the pavement. I'm encouraged when I see young, gifted women supporting and encouraging each other to take on public roles. If we're going to make progress towards the goal of valuing both genders equally, women will need to find the courage to step into roles that may be unfamiliar. They will need to deal with the 'imposter syndrome' that says they are occupying a space where they really don't belong.

But if women need to do some unfamiliar things to challenge the way the world thinks, so do men. When I was in my 20s I really thought we would have the problem of gender inequality sorted in my lifetime. Now I'm less hopeful. The most significant thing men like me can do is quite simple, but also very challenging: get out of the way. It's the exact opposite of 'building your personal brand'. It might mean men turning down invitations to lead and recommending women who could do the job just as well. It might even mean saying no to a promotion at work, if the other candidate is female. Or it might be something as simple but radical as walking down the pavement more thoughtfully, to make space for women to walk in straight lines.

The three things that characterize an Everyday Activist are faith, hope and mischief. By faith, I mean deciding to believe that there is a big picture that governs history. The opposite of faith is not doubt. Faith and doubt play for the same team. The opposite of faith is cynicism, which is to be avoided at all costs. By hope, I mean choosing to believe that, despite a lot of the evidence to the contrary, the world's story is going to end well. The opposite of hope is not pessimism. Pessimism may well be the most realistic stance in any given situation. The opposite of hope is giving up. I'm not giving up. By mischief, I mean that instead of being immobilized by my impotence or insignificance, I look for creative, joyful, cheeky, unorthodox ways to shift the status quo.

I am an Everyday Activist, and this is my creed: I believe in the power of tiny acts to change the world. I believe in taking risks, making trouble, and doing small things that make a big difference. I believe in walking under ladders, treading on the cracks in the pavement, and singing into the wind. I believe in bursting bubbles and poking fun at the over-mighty, especially if the over-mighty is myself. I'm not all-powerful, so that I can solve the world's problems, or even my own problems. But I'm not completely powerless either. There are things that I can do. I can't take responsibility for everything – not in my work, not in my community and not in my family, but that doesn't mean I have to wash my hands of everything either, as if it doesn't matter what I do. I am imperfect, but I'm not useless. I am an Everyday Activist. I am not everything that I could be, but I am not nothing either. Somewhere in between those two false ideals is the place where I live.